W

Causes of World War II
Allied Powers & Leaders
Axis Powers & Leaders of WW II
World War II in Europe
World War II in the Pacific
Technology in World War II
The US Home Front in WW II
Adolf Hitler
Benito Mussolini
Emperor Hirohito
Franklin D. Roosevelt
Harry S. Truman
Winston Churchill
Joseph Stalin
Admiral Bull Halsey
Admiral Nimitz
Admiral Nagumo
Admiral Yamamoto
General Douglas MacArthur
General Dwight D. Eisenhower
General George Patton
General Erwin Rommel
General Charles de Gaulle
Audie Murphy
Richard "Dick" Best
Wade McClusky
Heinrich Himmler
Josef Goebbels
Josef Mengele
African Americans in World War II
Daniel "Chappie" James
Dorie Miller
761st Tank Battalion
92nd Infantry Division
Tuskegee Airmen
The 1st Special Service Force in World War II

101st Airborne
Easy Company
Nurses of Pearl Harbor
Merrill's Marauders
Gurkha Troops
Navajo Code Talkers
Nisei Soldiers
The Ghost Army
French Resistance
Hitler Youth Program
German Panzer Divisions
The German Gestapo
The SS (Schutzstaffel)
Waffen-SS
Spies & Secret Agents of WW II
Attack on Pearl Harbor
Doolittle Raid
Bataan Death March
Battle of Britain
Battle of the Denmark Strait
Battle of Midway
Battle of Stalingrad
Battle of Guadalcanal
Battle of the Atlantic
D-Day
Attack on Pointe du Hoc
Battle of Ramree Island
Battle of Iwo Jima
Battle of the Bulge
Siege of Bastogne
Battle of Berlin
Hiroshima and Nagasaki
Sinking of the Indianapolis
The Holocaust
The Final Solution
Kristallnacht
The Zegota
Irena Sendler
Anne Frank

Auschwitz
Daily Life in Auschwitz
Liberation of Auschwitz
Importance of Remembering Auschwitz
The Liberation of the Nazi Death Train
The Warsaw Zoo
V-E Day
V-J Day
Nuremberg Trials
Recovery and the Marshall Plan
Aircraft Carriers
Role of Aircraft in World War II
B-17 Flying Fortress
Enola Gay
The Luftwaffe
The British Spitfire
German ME-262 Fighter
Japanese Zero
P-51 Mustang
Battleship Bismarck
Battleship Yamato
U.S.S. Arizona
U.S.S Iowa
U.S.S New Jersey
German Submarine Wolfpack
The Sherman Tank
The Tiger Tank
British A22 Churchill Tank
Japanese Type 97 Chi-Ha Tank
Soviet T-34 Tank
The Eagles Nest
The Enigma Machine
Shoichi Yokoi
Japanese Internment Camps

Copyright © 2024 JFBonham
All rights reserved. No part of this book may be reproduced, distributed, or transmitted in any form or by any means, including photocopying, recording, or other electronic or mechanical methods, without the prior written permission of JFBonham, except in the case of brief quotations embodied in critical reviews and certain other noncommercial uses permitted by copyright law.
Unauthorized use or reproduction of this workbook may result in legal action.

World War II: Overview

World War II was a monumental global conflict that took place from 1939 to 1945, involving many countries and leading to significant changes in the world. It began when Germany, led by Adolf Hitler, invaded Poland, prompting Britain and France to declare war on Germany. The war quickly escalated as more countries joined in, forming two major alliances: the Allies, led by the United States, the Soviet Union, and the United Kingdom, and the Axis, led by Germany, Japan, and Italy.

The war was fought on multiple fronts, spanning Europe, Asia, Africa, and the Pacific. It featured a range of strategies and technologies, from traditional infantry battles to air raids and naval conflicts. The conflict led to immense suffering and loss of life, affecting civilians and soldiers alike.

One of the most devastating aspects of World War II was the Holocaust, a systematic genocide perpetrated by the Nazis against six million Jews and millions of others. Concentration camps were established for mass extermination, and the world was horrified by the extent of the atrocities committed.

In Europe, the war witnessed iconic battles like the Battle of Stalingrad, where the Soviet Union halted the German advance and turned the tide of the war on the Eastern Front. Meanwhile, the Allied forces launched a massive invasion of Normandy, known as D-Day, in 1944. This operation led to the liberation of Western Europe from Nazi control.

In the Pacific theater, Japan's aggressive expansion led to conflicts with the United States. The attack on Pearl Harbor in 1941 prompted the U.S. to enter the war. The Pacific battles were characterized by island-hopping campaigns, where Allied forces gradually recaptured Japanese-held islands. The war in the Pacific culminated in the dropping of two atomic bombs on the Japanese cities of Hiroshima and Nagasaki in 1945, leading to Japan's surrender.

During the war, civilians on all sides endured great hardships. Cities were bombed, infrastructure was destroyed, and rationing became commonplace. The war effort required significant sacrifices from ordinary citizens, and women played a crucial role in the workforce, filling jobs traditionally held by men.

As the war neared its end, Allied leaders convened to plan the post-war world. The United Nations was established to promote international cooperation and prevent future conflicts. The war's aftermath led to the Cold War, a geopolitical tension between the United States and the Soviet Union, which shaped global politics for decades.

World War II concluded in 1945 with the unconditional surrender of Germany and Japan. The conflict had profound consequences, reshaping national borders, leading to the emergence of the United States and the Soviet Union as superpowers, and inspiring efforts to promote peace and human rights.

In conclusion, World War II was a monumental and tragic conflict that shaped the course of history. It brought together nations in a struggle for freedom and justice against oppressive forces. The war's impact on societies, politics, and culture continues to be felt to this day, reminding us of the importance of striving for peace and cooperation in the face of adversity.

Allied Powers & Leaders of WW II

During World War II, the Allied Powers were a coalition of countries united against the Axis Powers. These nations, led by influential leaders, played a crucial role in defeating the aggressors and restoring peace to the world.

The principal leaders of the Allied Powers were:

1. **United States - President Franklin D. Roosevelt:** Roosevelt, with his steady leadership and determination, guided the United States through much of the war until his death in 1945. He provided support to the Allies through the Lend-Lease Act, aiding them with military supplies and equipment.
2. **United Kingdom - Prime Minister Winston Churchill:** Known for his eloquence and unwavering resolve, Churchill rallied the British people during the darkest days of the war. His powerful speeches and strong leadership inspired the nation to persevere against Nazi aggression.
3. **Soviet Union - Premier Joseph Stalin:** Stalin led the Soviet Union during its epic struggle against Nazi Germany on the Eastern Front. Despite initial setbacks, his leadership and the resilience of the Soviet people played a decisive role in the Allies' victory.
4. **China - Generalissimo Chiang Kai-shek:** Chiang led China's resistance against the Japanese invasion. His determination to fight against overwhelming odds made China a significant contributor to the Allied cause in the Pacific theater.
5. **Free France - General Charles de Gaulle:** De Gaulle, as the leader of Free France, rallied French resistance against Nazi occupation and worked closely with the Allies to liberate France from German control.

As the war progressed, other countries joined the Allied Powers, including Canada, Australia, New Zealand, and various nations from Europe, Africa, and the Caribbean.

Together, they formed a formidable force against the Axis Powers.

The Allied Powers coordinated their military strategies and resources to defeat their common enemies. Key military campaigns included the D-Day invasion of Normandy in June 1944, known as Operation Overlord, which marked a significant turning point in the European theater. In the Pacific, the Allied forces successfully launched island-hopping campaigns to liberate territories from Japanese control.

The leaders of the Allied Powers worked together through conferences, such as the Tehran Conference in 1943 and the Yalta Conference in 1945, to plan their collective efforts and establish post-war goals. These conferences also laid the groundwork for the formation of the United Nations, a new international organization aimed at preventing future conflicts and promoting global cooperation.

Ultimately, the unity and determination of the Allied Powers, led by their visionary leaders, were instrumental in the defeat of the Axis Powers and the restoration of peace. Their collaboration and sacrifice during World War II laid the foundation for a new era of international cooperation and diplomacy.

Axis Powers & Leaders of WW II

During World War II, the Axis Powers were a coalition of countries that opposed the Allied Powers, led by Nazi Germany, Imperial Japan, and Fascist Italy. These nations sought to expand their territories and impose their ideologies on other parts of the world. The Axis Powers were unified in their goal to establish a new world order under their control, challenging the existing international order and causing immense devastation during the war.

Nazi Germany, led by Adolf Hitler, was the driving force behind the Axis Powers. Hitler rose to power in 1933 and aggressively pursued expansionist policies, seeking to establish a Greater German Empire through the annexation of neighboring territories. His ambition to establish a dominant Aryan race and eliminate what he perceived as inferior races led to the genocide of millions of Jews and other minority groups in the Holocaust.

Imperial Japan, under Emperor Hirohito and militaristic leadership, sought to create a Japanese-dominated East Asia. The Japanese expansionism in the 1930s and 1940s led to brutal invasions and occupations of neighboring countries, resulting in widespread atrocities and suffering.

Fascist Italy, led by Benito Mussolini, sought to establish a revived Roman Empire by expanding its territories across Europe and Africa. Mussolini's alliance with Hitler in 1939 formalized the Axis Powers and further solidified their collaboration.

These three countries formed the core of the Axis Powers, but other nations, such as Hungary, Romania, Bulgaria, and Finland, also joined the coalition to align with the Axis ideologies and territorial ambitions.

The Axis Powers coordinated their military efforts and resources during World War II, launching invasions and offensives against the Allied Powers. They achieved early successes, with Germany's Blitzkrieg tactics leading to swift victories in Europe and Japan's expansion across Asia and the Pacific.

However, as the war progressed, the tide began to turn against the Axis Powers. The Allied forces, comprising nations such as the United States, the Soviet Union, the United Kingdom, and others, mounted a determined resistance and launched counteroffensives that pushed back the Axis advances.

In 1945, the defeat of the Axis Powers was all but certain. Germany's surrender in May 1945, followed by Japan's surrender in September after the atomic bombings of Hiroshima and Nagasaki, marked the end of World War II and the downfall of the Axis Powers.

The Axis Powers and their leaders left a lasting legacy of destruction, suffering, and human rights abuses during World War II. The war resulted in the loss of millions of lives and left a profound impact on global politics and international relations. The defeat of the Axis Powers ultimately led to the establishment of new international organizations, such as the United Nations, to promote peace and prevent such catastrophic conflicts in the future.

World War II in Europe

The European Theater during World War II was a pivotal and intense battleground where the Allied forces, led by countries such as the United States, United Kingdom, and the Soviet Union, confronted the Axis powers, primarily Nazi Germany. This theater of war encompassed the vast landscapes of Europe, from the shores of Normandy to the Eastern Front, and played a crucial role in shaping the outcome of the war.

One of the most significant events in the European Theater was the D-Day invasion, which occurred on June 6, 1944. Allied forces launched a massive amphibious assault on the beaches of Normandy, France, in a bid to establish a foothold on the continent and begin the liberation of Western Europe from Nazi control. This operation marked a turning point as the Allies gained a vital position from which they could push further into Europe.

The Eastern Front was another critical arena in the European Theater. Nazi Germany's invasion of the Soviet Union in 1941 led to a brutal and protracted conflict. The harsh winters and vast expanses of land presented challenges to both sides. The Soviet Union's determination and the infamous Russian winter played a pivotal role in stalling the German advance. The Battle of Stalingrad, a gruesome and pivotal engagement, resulted in a decisive Soviet victory, turning the tide of the war on the Eastern Front.

In 1944, the Allies launched Operation Market Garden, an ambitious plan to secure key bridges in the Netherlands and pave the way for a swift advance into Germany. Despite initial successes, the operation ultimately fell short of its goals, highlighting the complexities and challenges of warfare in the European Theater.

As the Allies continued to push eastward, they faced fierce resistance from German forces. The Battle of the Bulge, which occurred in the Ardennes region in late 1944, was a surprise German counteroffensive aimed at dividing the Allied forces.

While the battle resulted in heavy casualties on both sides, the Allies managed to repel the German advance, further weakening the Nazi war machine.

The European Theater witnessed the liberation of concentration camps as Allied forces uncovered the horrors of the Holocaust. The discovery of these camps highlighted the atrocities committed by the Nazis and underscored the importance of defeating them. The Allies' commitment to defeating the Axis powers was further solidified by these revelations.

In the closing months of the war, Soviet forces launched a massive offensive on the Eastern Front, eventually reaching Berlin in April 1945. The Battle of Berlin marked the final stages of the European Theater, as Soviet troops encircled and captured the German capital. With Adolf Hitler's suicide and the fall of Berlin, Germany's surrender became imminent.

The European Theater of World War II was a complex and multifaceted arena that saw numerous battles, strategies, and sacrifices. It showcased the resilience of nations united against a common enemy and demonstrated the importance of coordination among Allied forces. The theater's outcome ultimately paved the way for the defeat of Nazi Germany and the restoration of peace to a war-torn continent.

World War II in the Pacific

The Pacific Theater of World War II was a vast and challenging battleground that stretched across the Pacific Ocean, involving countries like the United States, Japan, Australia, and many others. This theater witnessed intense battles, island-hopping campaigns, and naval clashes that shaped the outcome of the war.

At the heart of the Pacific Theater was the conflict between the United States and Japan. Tensions between the two nations had been simmering for years, and the attack on Pearl Harbor in December 1941 marked the beginning of full-scale warfare in the Pacific. The Pacific battles were unique due to the vast distances and the diverse range of terrain, from tropical islands to dense jungles.

Naval power played a pivotal role in the Pacific. The Battle of Midway, a turning point, saw the United States defeat the Japanese navy and gain the upper hand. Aircraft carriers became essential in this theater, serving as mobile air bases to launch airstrikes against distant targets. The Pacific also witnessed the infamous battles of Guadalcanal, Iwo Jima, and Okinawa, where fierce ground battles were fought for control of key islands.

One of the most iconic events was the "island-hopping" strategy employed by the Allies. This involved capturing specific islands while bypassing others, creating stepping stones toward Japan. This strategy allowed the Allies to establish airfields, supply bases, and strategic positions to launch further attacks. The Battle of Guadalcanal exemplified this approach, as American forces fought to secure the island and its airfield, denying the Japanese a critical staging point.

The harsh environment and unfamiliar terrain posed significant challenges to both sides. Jungle warfare became a defining aspect, with soldiers contending with dense forests, swamps, and harsh weather. The Battle of Peleliu showcased the grueling nature of such battles, as American forces fought to capture a small but heavily fortified island.

The Pacific Theater also highlighted the importance of amphibious assaults. Soldiers had to transition from naval vessels to the beaches, often facing fierce resistance from entrenched defenders. The Battle of Tarawa, in which U.S. Marines fought to seize a tiny island, demonstrated the challenges of storming well-fortified beaches.

The Pacific Theater was marked by the courage and determination of soldiers on both sides. The Japanese soldiers, known for their dedication to their emperor, employed defensive tactics that made capturing islands difficult. However, over time, the superior industrial and technological capabilities of the United States and its allies gave them the edge.

As the war progressed, the devastating power of atomic bombs came to the forefront. The decision to drop atomic bombs on Hiroshima and Nagasaki brought about Japan's surrender and the end of World War II. The Pacific Theater left an indelible mark on history, demonstrating the importance of naval power, island warfare, and innovative strategies in shaping the course of a war.

In conclusion, the Pacific Theater of World War II was a complex and dynamic arena that saw intense battles, innovative strategies, and a wide range of challenges. The battles fought across vast oceans and on remote islands showcased the resilience and determination of those who fought in this theater. The Pacific campaigns ultimately played a pivotal role in bringing about the end of the war and reshaping the world order.

Technology in World War II

World War II was a time of big changes in how wars were fought. New technologies made a big difference in how countries fought and how they communicated.

One important technology was radar. Radar uses radio waves to find objects far away, even in the dark or bad weather. During the war, radar helped countries spot enemy planes and ships. This made it easier to defend against surprise attacks and plan better strategies.

Another key technology was sonar. Sonar uses sound waves to find things underwater, like submarines. With sonar, ships could find hidden submarines and protect themselves. This helped keep the seas safer for the ships and the people on them.

Aircraft also changed a lot during the war. Bombers could now fly farther and carry bigger bombs. This meant they could hit targets deep in enemy territory. Fighter planes got faster and more maneuverable, making air battles more intense. New planes, like the American P-51 Mustang, had longer ranges and could protect bombers on their missions.

Communication was a big challenge, but new technologies helped a lot. Walkie-talkies and portable radios let soldiers and leaders talk to each other even when they were far apart. This helped troops coordinate better on the battlefield. Plus, codebreakers were able to figure out secret enemy messages, which gave the Allies an advantage.

Medical care improved too. Penicillin, a new medicine, helped treat infections and saved many lives. Doctors also used mobile X-ray machines to find injuries inside soldiers' bodies. Blood transfusions became more common, which helped wounded soldiers get the blood they needed to survive.

Tanks were another vital technology. They became more powerful and better protected. Tanks could move across rough terrain and take out enemy defenses. This changed how battles were fought on land, making tanks a crucial part of many strategies.

In cities, people had to use blackout curtains and shelters to protect themselves from air raids. But even on the home front, technology made a difference. Factories used machines to build weapons and supplies quickly. Women played a big role in these factories, showing that everyone could help in the war effort.

After the war, many of these technologies continued to improve and shape the world. Radar became useful for weather forecasting and air travel. Sonar helped with ocean exploration and navigation. Computers, which were used to crack codes, became faster and more powerful, leading to the computers we use today. Medical advances from the war saved lives and changed how doctors treated patients.

In conclusion, World War II brought about a wave of new technologies that changed how wars were fought and how people communicated. Radar and sonar helped spot enemies, aircraft got faster and more powerful, and communication became easier with radios. Medical care improved with new medicines and techniques. All of these advancements had a lasting impact on the world, making it safer, more connected, and more technologically advanced.

The US Home Front in WW II

During World War II, the United States underwent a profound transformation on the home front. As the nation mobilized for war, every aspect of American society was impacted, from the economy and industry to daily life and social norms. The US home front played an essential role in supporting the war effort, with citizens uniting behind a common cause to ensure victory against the Axis powers.

The US home front during World War II was characterized by unprecedented levels of patriotism, unity, and shared sacrifice. As millions of American soldiers and sailors fought overseas, those on the home front rallied to support them and contribute to the war effort. Factories that once produced consumer goods shifted their focus to manufacturing tanks, planes, ships, and weaponry needed for the war. This transition was facilitated by the federal government's establishment of agencies like the War Production Board, which oversaw the efficient allocation of resources for military production.

Women played a critical role in the war effort, joining the workforce in unprecedented numbers to fill roles traditionally held by men. With men serving in the armed forces, women took up jobs in factories, offices, and other industries. The iconic image of "Rosie the Riveter" symbolized the millions of women who contributed to the production of war materials, effectively becoming the backbone of the US war economy. This shift in gender roles had a lasting impact on women's rights and opportunities in the decades that followed.

Rationing and conservation became integral aspects of life on the US home front. The government implemented rationing programs to ensure that essential goods like food, fuel, and rubber were allocated fairly and efficiently. Citizens received ration coupons to purchase limited quantities of goods. These measures aimed to prevent shortages and redirect resources to the military. Additionally, citizens participated in scrap drives to collect materials like metal, paper, and rubber for recycling and reuse in war production.

Propaganda played a significant role in shaping public perception and encouraging participation in the war effort. Posters, films, and advertisements depicted patriotic themes and encouraged citizens to buy war bonds, conserve resources, and support the troops. These efforts fostered a sense of unity and duty among the American population, emphasizing the importance of individual contributions to the collective cause.

Civilian defense programs were established to protect American cities from potential enemy attacks. Air raid drills and blackout measures were conducted to prepare citizens for the possibility of air raids. Neighborhoods organized volunteer air raid wardens, blackout committees, and first aid teams to ensure community safety during times of heightened threat.

The war effort on the US home front extended beyond the tangible contributions of goods and labor. Entertainment played a role in boosting morale, with Hollywood producing films that inspired and entertained audiences while promoting patriotic values. Additionally, celebrities and performers embarked on USO tours to entertain troops stationed both domestically and abroad.

Adolf Hitler

Adolf Hitler's rise to power and his role in World War II are pivotal chapters in history that shaped the 20th century. Born in Austria in 1889, Hitler's early life was marked by struggles and aspirations as an artist. However, his deep-rooted anti-Semitic and nationalist beliefs eventually led him on a path that would reshape the world.

Hitler's entry into politics occurred in the aftermath of World War I. The harsh terms of the Treaty of Versailles imposed on Germany fueled national resentment and economic hardship. In this climate of discontent, Hitler found a platform for his extremist ideas. He joined the German Workers' Party, which he later renamed the National Socialist German Workers' Party (Nazi Party). His charismatic speeches and promises of restoring Germany's greatness resonated with many who sought a way out of their dire circumstances.

As Hitler rose within the Nazi Party, his vision of Aryan supremacy, anti-Semitism, and expansionism gained traction. In 1933, he became the Chancellor of Germany, capitalizing on political maneuvering and exploiting the Reichstag fire to consolidate power. Within months, he orchestrated the Enabling Act, effectively granting him dictatorial authority. Hitler's ascendancy marked the beginning of a totalitarian regime that would lead to profound consequences.

One of Hitler's first acts as Chancellor was to dismantle democratic institutions, suppress dissent, and eliminate political opponents. The Gestapo, the secret police force, played a central role in these efforts, using fear and intimidation to silence any opposition. Hitler's propaganda machine further manipulated public opinion, promoting his ideas of racial purity and aggressive expansion.

Hitler's foreign policy revolved around overturning the Treaty of Versailles and expanding Germany's territories. His ambitions led to the remilitarization of the Rhineland, the annexation of Austria (Anschluss), and the occupation of the

Sudetenland in Czechoslovakia. These actions, met with limited international resistance, emboldened Hitler to push further.

The apex of Hitler's aggressive expansionist policies was the invasion of Poland in September 1939. This marked the beginning of World War II, as Britain and France declared war on Germany in response. Hitler's military strategies, particularly the blitzkrieg, showcased his tactical prowess and initially led to sweeping victories across Europe. France fell in 1940, and Hitler turned his attention to the Soviet Union, launching Operation Barbarossa in 1941.

However, Hitler's overconfidence and strategic errors began to unravel his conquests. The Soviet Union's resilience and the entrance of the United States into the war shifted the tide. The brutality of Hitler's regime became increasingly evident, especially with the implementation of the Holocaust, the systematic genocide of six million Jews and millions of others.

By 1945, the war had taken a devastating toll on Germany and its occupied territories. As Allied forces closed in, Hitler's grasp on reality seemed to waver. Refusing to acknowledge defeat, he retreated to his underground bunker in Berlin. On April 30, 1945, with Soviet forces at the city's doorstep, Hitler took his own life.

Benito Mussolini

Benito Mussolini, an Italian leader during World War II, played a significant role that greatly impacted the course of the war. Mussolini was the leader of Italy and a founding figure of fascism, a political ideology that championed extreme nationalism, militarism, and authoritarian rule. His actions and decisions had far-reaching consequences that influenced the outcome of the war.

Mussolini rose to power in the 1920s, establishing a regime that aimed to restore Italy's greatness and prominence on the world stage. In the years leading up to World War II, Mussolini aligned Italy with Nazi Germany and Japan, forming the Axis powers. This alliance aimed to challenge the influence of the Allied powers, which included countries like the United States, the United Kingdom, and the Soviet Union.

Mussolini's involvement in World War II began with his expansionist ambitions. He sought to increase Italy's territorial holdings and influence by engaging in aggressive military campaigns. In 1935, Italy invaded Ethiopia, a country in East Africa, seeking to establish a colonial empire. This invasion was met with international condemnation, but it also set the stage for Italy's further militaristic actions.

As tensions escalated in Europe, Mussolini saw an opportunity to expand Italy's territory. In 1939, he invaded Albania, a smaller neighboring country, with little resistance. However, his ambitions extended beyond Albania. Mussolini sought to claim territories that he believed were historically Italian, such as parts of France and the Balkans. In 1940, Italy entered World War II on the side of Nazi Germany.

Mussolini's decision to join the war proved to be ill-fated. Italy's military was ill-prepared and lacked the resources to effectively contribute to the war effort. Italian forces suffered significant defeats, notably in North Africa, where they were pitted against the skilled British forces led by General Bernard

Montgomery. The Italian military's failures weakened the Axis powers' position in the war.

One of Mussolini's most notorious decisions during the war was his invasion of Greece in 1940. Despite assurances from Hitler that Germany would support the campaign, the Italian forces faced strong Greek resistance and were eventually pushed back. This compelled Germany to intervene and launch its own invasion of Greece, diverting valuable resources from the Eastern Front.

By 1943, the tide of the war had turned against the Axis powers. The Allied forces made significant advancements, and Italy faced internal turmoil. Mussolini's leadership was increasingly challenged, and he was even arrested by his own government. In a dramatic turn of events, Mussolini was rescued by German forces and established a puppet state in Northern Italy under German control.

Mussolini's puppet government, known as the Italian Social Republic, was short-lived. As the Allied forces closed in, Mussolini's regime crumbled. He was captured by Italian partisans in 1945 and executed. Mussolini's role in World War II ultimately ended in failure and disgrace.

Emperor Hirohito

Emperor Hirohito played a significant role during World War II, serving as the symbolic leader of Japan. His role was marked by a complex blend of tradition, authority, and influence within the Japanese government and society.

Hirohito ascended to the Chrysanthemum Throne in 1926, becoming the 124th Emperor of Japan. As Emperor, he held a revered position in Japanese culture, representing the continuity of the nation's ancient traditions. During World War II, Hirohito's role was primarily as a figurehead, as Japan's political and military decisions were largely controlled by a group of military leaders and politicians.

One of the most notable aspects of Hirohito's role during the war was his endorsement of Japan's aggressive expansionist policies. The Japanese military sought to establish dominance in the Asia-Pacific region, which led to the invasion of China in 1937 and later conflicts with the United States and other Allied powers. Hirohito's imperial position lent legitimacy to these actions, as his symbolic approval was used to justify Japan's actions to the Japanese people.

However, Hirohito's level of direct involvement in military decision-making is a subject of historical debate. Some historians argue that he was a more passive participant, while others suggest that he had a more active role in shaping certain aspects of Japan's wartime strategy. Regardless of the extent of his involvement, his symbolic importance remained undeniable.

As World War II progressed, Japan faced increasing challenges and setbacks. The bombings of Hiroshima and Nagasaki by the United States in August 1945 finally forced Japan's surrender. In a radio address on August 15, 1945, Hirohito announced Japan's unconditional surrender to the Allied powers. This marked a significant turning point, as Hirohito's voice carried immense weight in Japanese society, and his announcement signaled the end of the war and the beginning of Japan's reconstruction.

After Japan's surrender, Hirohito's role underwent a transformation. The Allied occupation, led by General Douglas MacArthur, implemented democratic reforms in Japan. Hirohito cooperated with the occupation forces, renouncing his divine status and expressing remorse for the war. This move helped pave the way for Japan's transition to a constitutional monarchy with limited political power for the emperor.

In the years following World War II, Hirohito's role shifted from that of a powerful figurehead to a symbol of Japan's post-war transformation and reconciliation with the international community. He continued to reign as Emperor until his death in 1989, witnessing Japan's remarkable recovery and transformation into an economic powerhouse while maintaining his largely ceremonial position.

In conclusion, Emperor Hirohito's role during World War II was marked by his symbolic significance as the leader of Japan, even though his actual influence on political and military decisions was limited. His endorsement of Japan's wartime actions lent legitimacy to its expansionist policies, and his post-war cooperation with the Allied occupation contributed to Japan's transition into a modern constitutional monarchy. Hirohito's reign encompassed both a period of militarism and conflict and a subsequent era of rebuilding and reconciliation.

Franklin D. Roosevelt

Franklin D. Roosevelt, the 32nd President of the United States, played a pivotal role in leading his nation through the challenges and complexities of World War II. His leadership, strategic acumen, and diplomatic finesse were instrumental in guiding the United States to victory and shaping the post-war world order.

As the world was engulfed in conflict in the late 1930s, President Roosevelt's initial focus was on maintaining American neutrality while closely monitoring international developments. However, his awareness of the growing threat posed by Nazi Germany and its aggressive expansionist policies prompted him to take steps to bolster national defense and aid countries facing Axis aggression.

In 1940, Roosevelt championed the Lend-Lease Act, which allowed the United States to provide military equipment and supplies to Allied nations without entering the war. This policy enabled the U.S. to support its allies while avoiding direct military involvement. Roosevelt's foresight in recognizing the importance of assisting democratic nations under attack showcased his commitment to the principles of freedom and democracy.

The course of history took a definitive turn on December 7, 1941, when Japan's surprise attack on the U.S. naval base at Pearl Harbor propelled the United States into World War II. In response, Roosevelt delivered his famous "Day of Infamy" speech to Congress, galvanizing the nation's resolve to confront the Axis powers head-on. This marked the beginning of Roosevelt's active engagement in the war effort.

Throughout the war, President Roosevelt's leadership was characterized by his ability to build and maintain strong alliances with other Allied leaders. His partnership with British Prime Minister Winston Churchill was particularly notable. Together, they forged a close bond and worked to develop a unified strategy against the Axis powers. The two leaders met multiple times to discuss military plans, share intelligence, and solidify their commitment to victory.

Roosevelt's role extended beyond military matters. He played a crucial role in planning and establishing the United Nations, an international organization aimed at promoting peace and cooperation among nations. His vision for a post-war world order that prevented future global conflicts led to the signing of the United Nations Declaration in 1942.

On the home front, President Roosevelt skillfully managed the American economy's transition to a wartime footing. He oversaw the rapid mobilization of industries for war production, which provided essential equipment, weapons, and supplies for the military. The war effort not only lifted the country out of the Great Depression but also created millions of jobs, transforming the American economy.

Roosevelt's leadership also extended to the delicate issue of civil rights and social justice. He issued Executive Order 8802, which prohibited racial discrimination in defense industries and marked a step towards greater equality. While challenges remained, this action laid the groundwork for future civil rights advancements.

Tragically, President Roosevelt did not live to witness the end of the war. He passed away on April 12, 1945, just months before victory in Europe was achieved. His Vice President, Harry S. Truman, assumed the presidency and carried forward the final stages of the war.

Harry S. Truman

Harry S. Truman, the 33rd President of the United States, played a crucial role in World War II that extended from his early days as a senator to his unexpected ascendancy to the presidency. As a key decision-maker during this tumultuous period, Truman's actions and leadership significantly influenced the outcome of the war and the subsequent shaping of the post-war world order.

Truman's involvement in World War II began well before he assumed the presidency. As a U.S. Senator from Missouri, he was appointed to oversee the Truman Committee in 1941. This committee was tasked with investigating war production and expenditures to ensure efficiency and prevent waste. Truman's oversight of defense contracts and military spending not only contributed to the war effort but also earned him a reputation as a diligent and responsible legislator.

In April 1945, the unexpected passing of President Franklin D. Roosevelt thrust Truman into the presidency. At that time, World War II was reaching its climactic stages, with Allied forces advancing on multiple fronts. Truman was immediately faced with monumental decisions, including the use of the newly developed atomic bomb.

One of the most defining moments of Truman's presidency and his role in World War II was the decision to drop atomic bombs on the Japanese cities of Hiroshima and Nagasaki in August 1945. Truman's choice was driven by the belief that such drastic measures would hasten Japan's surrender, potentially saving countless lives that would be lost in a prolonged invasion of Japan. The bombings ultimately led to Japan's surrender and the end of World War II, but they also ignited debates about the ethical implications of using nuclear weapons.

Truman's leadership extended beyond military decisions. He was instrumental in shaping the post-war world order through his involvement in the creation of the United Nations.

Attending the Potsdam Conference in 1945 alongside Allied leaders Winston Churchill and Joseph Stalin, Truman helped negotiate terms for the defeated Axis powers and laid the groundwork for the establishment of the United Nations, an international organization aimed at promoting peace and cooperation among nations.

Furthermore, Truman's policies aimed at rebuilding Europe through the Marshall Plan demonstrated his commitment to global stability after the war. The plan provided financial aid to war-torn European countries, aiding in their recovery and preventing the spread of communism. Truman recognized that economic stability was essential to prevent the resurgence of conflicts that had led to two devastating world wars.

Truman's role in World War II was characterized by his leadership during a critical transition period. He guided the nation from the war's conclusion to the challenges of post-war reconstruction and the complexities of the emerging Cold War. Truman's commitment to international cooperation, as seen through his involvement in the United Nations and the Marshall Plan, reflected his vision for a more peaceful and stable world.

Winston Churchill

Winston Churchill, a charismatic and resolute leader, played a pivotal role in World War II as the Prime Minister of the United Kingdom. His steadfast determination and stirring speeches rallied the British people and inspired Allied forces to withstand the challenges of war. From 1940 to 1945, Churchill's leadership proved instrumental in guiding his nation through the tumultuous times of conflict.

As the war engulfed Europe and the threat of Nazi Germany loomed large, Churchill assumed office on May 10, 1940. His unwavering resolve quickly became apparent when, facing the daunting prospect of a German invasion, he delivered his famous speech: "We shall fight on the beaches, we shall fight on the landing grounds, we shall fight in the fields and in the streets, we shall fight in the hills; we shall never surrender." This resolute commitment to resistance boosted morale and united the British people in their determination to thwart the Nazi onslaught.

Churchill's strategic insights and strong leadership abilities were evident during significant events such as the Battle of Britain. As German air raids pounded Britain's cities, he supported the Royal Air Force's valiant defense, which ultimately halted Germany's aerial campaign. Churchill's leadership in this critical phase of the war helped maintain British control of the skies and prevented a German invasion.

Another pivotal moment came with the evacuation of Allied forces from the beaches of Dunkirk in 1940. Despite the retreat, Churchill's leadership framed the operation as a "miracle of deliverance," highlighting the successful rescue of over 330,000 British and French soldiers and bolstering national pride.

Churchill's role extended beyond his own nation. He fostered strong relationships with key Allied leaders, notably U.S. President Franklin D. Roosevelt and Soviet Premier Joseph Stalin. These alliances formed the basis for the united front against the Axis powers. Together, they strategized and coordinated efforts to defeat Germany, Italy, and Japan.

Perhaps one of Churchill's most defining moments was his stirring support for the people of London during the Blitz. Despite the relentless bombing campaign, he stood alongside Londoners, visiting bombed areas, and showing his resilience in the face of adversity. His appearances boosted the city's morale and demonstrated his commitment to their safety and well-being.

Churchill's vision for a post-war world was reflected in his role in shaping the Atlantic Charter, a joint declaration with President Roosevelt that outlined principles for a more just and peaceful world order after the war's conclusion. This charter laid the groundwork for the establishment of the United Nations, an organization aimed at preventing future global conflicts.

In 1945, as World War II drew to a close, Churchill's Conservative Party faced defeat in the general election. Despite his immense wartime contributions, the British people opted for a Labour government. Churchill's tenure as Prime Minister came to an end, but his legacy as a steadfast leader during Britain's darkest hours remained undiminished.

Winston Churchill's role in World War II was characterized by his unyielding determination, eloquent rhetoric, and strong leadership qualities. Through his speeches, strategic decisions, and unwavering support for the British people, he inspired a nation and

Joseph Stalin

Joseph Stalin's role in World War II was marked by his leadership of the Soviet Union through the tumultuous and harrowing period of the conflict. As the head of the Soviet government, Stalin played a crucial role in the war effort, making strategic decisions that significantly impacted the course of the war and the eventual defeat of Nazi Germany.

Stalin's leadership during World War II was characterized by a mix of ruthless pragmatism and strategic acumen. He recognized the urgent need to defend the Soviet Union from the Nazi invasion and embarked on a strategy that combined military mobilization, propaganda, and industrial production on an unprecedented scale. Stalin's ability to mobilize the Soviet people and resources played a critical role in the eventual victory over the Axis powers.

One of Stalin's most significant contributions was his unwavering determination to resist the German invasion. When Operation Barbarossa was launched by Nazi Germany in June 1941, catching the Soviets off guard, Stalin quickly rallied the Soviet forces and the population. Despite initial setbacks, he galvanized the nation's resolve and inspired a fierce resistance that halted the German advance and turned the tide of the war on the Eastern Front.

Stalin's collaboration with the Allied powers, particularly the United States and the United Kingdom, was essential in coordinating a unified effort against the Axis forces. The Tehran Conference in 1943, where Stalin met with Winston Churchill and Franklin D. Roosevelt, solidified the Allies' commitment to cooperation and strategic planning. This collaboration helped shape major decisions, including the timing and location of major offensives, such as Operation Overlord, the Allied invasion of Normandy.

Stalin's influence extended to the Eastern Front, where he made key decisions about military strategy and the allocation of resources. He closely coordinated with his generals, including Georgy Zhukov, who played a pivotal role in planning and executing successful offensives against the German forces. Stalin's determination to liberate Soviet territory from occupation and to push the German forces back was evident in his approach to battles such as the Battle of Stalingrad, a turning point in the war that saw the encirclement and surrender of the German Sixth Army.

However, Stalin's leadership was not without controversy and brutality. His policies resulted in significant human suffering, including the purges of the 1930s, which targeted perceived enemies within the Soviet Union. The wartime period also saw the Soviet government's use of harsh measures, including mass deportations of certain ethnic groups, in response to potential collaboration with the Axis forces.

In terms of post-war diplomacy, Stalin's leadership had a profound impact on shaping the post-war world order. As the war drew to a close, he participated in the Yalta Conference alongside Churchill and Roosevelt, where agreements were made about the occupation and division of post-war Europe. The conference laid the groundwork for the division of Germany and the eventual emergence of the Cold War between the United States and the Soviet Union.

Joseph Stalin's role in World War II was characterized by his leadership of the Soviet Union through the challenging and complex period of the conflict. His mobilization of resources, determination to resist the German invasion, and collaboration with the Allies played a vital role in the eventual defeat of Nazi Germany. However, his leadership was also marked by controversial policies and decisions that had significant human and geopolitical consequences. Stalin's legacy in World War II remains a complex and debated topic, reflecting the complexities of leadership in times of great turmoil.

Admiral Bull Halsey

Admiral William "Bull" Halsey Jr. was a prominent and esteemed figure in American naval history, renowned for his leadership and valor during World War II. Born on October 30, 1882, in Elizabeth, New Jersey, Halsey joined the United States Naval Academy in 1900 and graduated in 1904. Over the years, he demonstrated exceptional capabilities as a naval officer, eventually rising to the rank of Admiral.

During World War II, Admiral Halsey played a significant role in the Pacific theater, commanding the Third Fleet. Known for his aggressive and tenacious tactics, he became a formidable adversary to the Japanese forces. His leadership style earned him the nickname "Bull" due to his forceful and straightforward demeanor.

One of Halsey's notable accomplishments during the war was his involvement in the Guadalcanal campaign. In 1942, he commanded the South Pacific Area, leading the Allied forces in the Battle of Guadalcanal. Despite challenges, Halsey's determination and strategic acumen contributed to the eventual Allied victory, securing a crucial foothold in the Solomon Islands.

During the Battle of Leyte Gulf in October 1944, Halsey's daring decision to pursue a decoy Japanese fleet left the Allied landing forces vulnerable to a surprise attack by the main Japanese force, known as the Battle of Samar. While his decision was controversial and drew criticism, Halsey's aggressive tactics were often credited with keeping the Japanese forces off balance and disrupting their plans.

As commander of the Third Fleet, Halsey led numerous naval operations, including the strikes on the Japanese home islands. His fleet played a vital role in weakening Japan's ability to wage war, delivering devastating airstrikes and contributing to the overall success of the Pacific campaign.

Halsey's leadership was also marked by his genuine concern for the welfare of his sailors. He earned the admiration and respect of his subordinates, who appreciated his hands-on approach and willingness to share their hardships.

After the war, Halsey continued to serve in various capacities within the U.S. Navy. He retired from active duty in 1947 but remained a prominent figure in the naval community and was actively involved in veterans' affairs.

Admiral William "Bull" Halsey's contributions to the Allied victory in the Pacific theater of World War II have left an enduring legacy. His strategic brilliance, audacity, and dedication to his sailors made him a revered figure among both his comrades and the American public. Despite the controversies surrounding some of his decisions, Halsey's role as a dynamic and determined naval leader solidifies his place as one of the greatest military commanders in American history. His legacy continues to inspire generations of naval officers and remains a testament to the courage and fortitude exhibited by the United States Navy during World War II.

Admiral Nimitz

Admiral Chester W. Nimitz, a legendary figure in American naval history, played a pivotal role in World War II as the commander of the U.S. Pacific Fleet. His strategic brilliance, leadership, and ability to adapt to rapidly changing situations made him one of the most successful naval commanders of the war.

Nimitz was born on February 24, 1885, in Fredericksburg, Texas. He entered the United States Naval Academy in 1901 and graduated in 1905. Over the years, he rose through the ranks and held various command positions, gaining valuable experience and earning a reputation as a capable and respected officer.

After the Japanese attack on Pearl Harbor on December 7, 1941, Nimitz was appointed as the Commander in Chief of the U.S. Pacific Fleet. He faced the daunting task of rebuilding and reorganizing the fleet after the devastating attack. Under his leadership, the U.S. Navy launched an intense effort to recover from the losses and rebuild its strength.

Nimitz's strategic vision was crucial in the Pacific theater. He recognized the importance of aircraft carriers and their potential in naval warfare. During the Battle of Midway in June 1942, Nimitz's decision to send the U.S. carriers to intercept the Japanese fleet proved decisive. The Americans inflicted a devastating defeat on the Japanese, sinking four of their aircraft carriers and shifting the balance of power in the Pacific.

Under Nimitz's command, the U.S. Navy engaged in a series of successful island-hopping campaigns in the Pacific, seizing key strategic locations and advancing towards Japan. His leadership during the battles of Guadalcanal,

Leyte Gulf, and Okinawa demonstrated his ability to coordinate and lead large-scale naval operations.

Nimitz's emphasis on decentralized command and his trust in subordinate commanders earned him the respect and loyalty of his officers and sailors. He believed in empowering his commanders to make decisions based on their assessment of the situation on the ground.

After the end of World War II, Nimitz played a crucial role in the formation of the United Nations and served as its Chief of Naval Operations. In 1947, he was promoted to the rank of Fleet Admiral, a five-star rank that was only awarded to five officers in U.S. history.

Admiral Chester W. Nimitz's legacy as a strategic genius and an exceptional naval leader endures to this day. His contributions to the U.S. victory in the Pacific theater of World War II and his unwavering commitment to his troops and the nation's security have solidified his place as one of the greatest military leaders in American history.

Admiral Nagumo

Admiral Isoroku Nagumo, a prominent figure in the history of the Imperial Japanese Navy during World War II, was renowned for his strategic brilliance and leadership prowess. Born on March 25, 1887, in the Yamagata Prefecture of Japan, Nagumo's military career began at the age of 18 when he enrolled in the Japanese Naval Academy. Throughout his impressive tenure, he became an instrumental figure in shaping Japan's naval forces, leaving an indelible mark on the nation's military history.

Nagumo's rise to prominence came in 1937 when he was appointed as a Rear Admiral and tasked with overseeing the 4th Carrier Division. His exceptional performance led to subsequent promotions, and by 1940, he attained the rank of Vice Admiral. As Japan's political climate shifted, the nation found itself on the brink of a global conflict. It was during this time that Nagumo received the responsibility that would forever etch his name in history.

In December 1941, the Imperial Japanese Navy executed a surprise attack on the United States' Pacific Fleet at Pearl Harbor, Hawaii. Admiral Nagumo spearheaded this audacious operation, codenamed "Operation AI," with meticulous planning and precision. The attack inflicted severe damage on the US Navy, temporarily crippling their Pacific forces and thrusting Japan into the heart of World War II.

One of Nagumo's defining traits was his ability to maintain composure in the face of adversity. His strategic brilliance and decisiveness were demonstrated during the Battle of Midway in June 1942, a critical turning point in the war. Despite the initial success of the Japanese in damaging the US aircraft carriers, Nagumo chose to change the armament of his aircraft, a decision that proved to be fateful.

Regrettably, Nagumo's cautious nature ultimately led to a missed opportunity at the Battle of Midway. After receiving conflicting reports of American carrier locations, he hesitated and delayed launching a second wave of attacks, allowing the US to mount a devastating counteroffensive. This tactical error turned the tide of the battle in favor of the United States, and Japan suffered a significant defeat, losing four of its aircraft carriers.

Nonetheless, Admiral Nagumo continued to be an influential commander. He played a vital role in defending Japanese-held territories during the Guadalcanal Campaign. His strategic acumen and determination ensured the effective use of the remaining Japanese naval assets.

Tragically, on July 6, 1944, Admiral Isoroku Nagumo's life came to an end. During the Battle of Saipan, an American planes attacked and sank his flagship, the battleship Yamato, causing him to take his own life. The loss of Nagumo was deeply felt in Japan, as he was considered one of the most accomplished and respected naval leaders of his time.

Admiral Isoroku Nagumo's legacy endures, marked by his strategic brilliance and dedication to the Imperial Japanese Navy. While the outcome of some of his decisions was contentious, his contributions to naval warfare cannot be understated. Nagumo's tactical skills, leadership, and unyielding commitment to his country have left an indelible imprint on Japan's military history and continue to be remembered to this day.

Admiral Yamamoto

Admiral Isoroku Yamamoto was a prominent Japanese naval officer during World War II, known for his strategic brilliance and key role in planning some of the most significant operations of the war. Born in 1884, Yamamoto joined the Imperial Japanese Navy at an early age and quickly rose through the ranks, becoming a vice-admiral by 1930.

Yamamoto's strategic acumen and deep understanding of naval warfare made him a respected figure among his peers. He was instrumental in developing the concept of "decisive battle" (kantai kessen), emphasizing the importance of a single decisive engagement to secure victory. His strategic vision led to the expansion of the Japanese Navy and the formation of the Combined Fleet.

One of Yamamoto's most well-known contributions was the planning and execution of the attack on Pearl Harbor on December 7, 1941. As the commander-in-chief of the Combined Fleet, he devised a daring plan to launch a surprise attack on the U.S. Pacific Fleet's base in Hawaii. The attack inflicted severe damage on the U.S. Navy and temporarily crippled American naval power in the Pacific.

Despite the success of the Pearl Harbor attack, Yamamoto was skeptical of the long-term prospects of Japan's war with the United States. He famously warned that Japan could win a few early battles but would ultimately struggle to defeat the United States in a prolonged conflict. Despite his reservations, he remained dedicated to his country's cause and continued to lead naval operations.

In 1943, Yamamoto's strategic focus shifted to the Solomon Islands campaign. He sought to draw the American fleet into a decisive battle near the island of Bougainville, hoping to inflict a major defeat on the U.S. Navy. However, U.S. intelligence intercepted and deciphered Japanese communications, learning of Yamamoto's travel plans. In April 1943, American fighter aircraft ambushed his plane during a trip to the Bougainville area, leading to his untimely death.

Yamamoto's death was a significant loss for the Japanese war effort. His strategic brilliance and leadership were unmatched, and he was a key figure in the planning of major naval operations. While his contributions to early Japanese victories were undeniable, his predictions about the challenges Japan would face in a prolonged war with the United States ultimately proved accurate.

In conclusion, Admiral Isoroku Yamamoto was a highly influential figure in World War II, responsible for planning critical naval operations for Japan. His strategic vision, particularly in the planning of the attack on Pearl Harbor, marked a turning point in the war. Despite his prowess, Yamamoto's life was tragically cut short, leaving Japan without his exceptional leadership during the later stages of the conflict. Nonetheless, his legacy as one of Japan's greatest naval commanders continues to be remembered and respected to this day.

General Douglas MacArthur

General Douglas MacArthur's role in World War II was marked by his strategic brilliance, unwavering leadership, and significant contributions to the Allied victory in the Pacific theater. As a highly skilled military commander, MacArthur played a vital role in shaping the course of the war and ensuring the success of Allied operations.

At the outbreak of World War II, General MacArthur was tasked with the defense of the Philippines, then a U.S. territory. Despite facing overwhelming odds due to the swift advance of Japanese forces, MacArthur displayed exceptional determination and resourcefulness. As the situation deteriorated, he famously declared, "I shall return," promising to come back and liberate the Philippines from Japanese occupation.

After the fall of the Philippines, MacArthur's leadership qualities came to the forefront as he was appointed as Supreme Commander of the Southwest Pacific Area. This role put him in charge of coordinating Allied operations across a vast region, including the Pacific islands. MacArthur's strategic planning and innovative tactics played a critical role in gradually rolling back Japanese advances.

One of the most notable achievements of General MacArthur's leadership was the campaign to retake the Philippines. In October 1944, he fulfilled his promise by leading a successful amphibious assault on the island of Leyte. This marked a turning point in the Pacific theater, as it enabled the U.S. to establish a foothold for further offensives against Japanese-held territories.

MacArthur's military acumen was evident in his planning of the island-hopping strategy. Instead of directly attacking heavily fortified Japanese strongholds, he opted to bypass some islands and seize strategically important ones, gradually isolating and weakening Japanese forces. This approach minimized casualties and expedited the advance towards Japan.

One of the most iconic moments of MacArthur's leadership came when he returned to the Philippines in 1945. Wading ashore at Leyte, he fulfilled his promise to liberate the country and delivered a memorable speech affirming the enduring friendship between the Philippines and the United States.

As the war approached its conclusion, General MacArthur was given the significant responsibility of planning the occupation of Japan. His leadership during the post-war period was instrumental in guiding Japan's transformation from a militaristic power to a democratic nation. MacArthur played a key role in drafting Japan's new constitution and implementing reforms that paved the way for its peaceful reintegration into the international community.

However, MacArthur's post-war leadership also drew controversy, particularly his clashes with U.S. government officials over policy decisions. His desire for a more aggressive approach towards China during the Korean War eventually led to his removal from command by President Harry S. Truman.

General Dwight D. Eisenhower

General Dwight D. Eisenhower, a towering figure in World War II, played a pivotal role as the Supreme Commander of the Allied Expeditionary Forces in Europe. His exceptional leadership, strategic prowess, and ability to forge international cooperation were instrumental in the success of the Allied efforts to liberate Europe from Nazi tyranny.

Eisenhower's prominence in the war effort was solidified when he was appointed Supreme Commander in January 1944. His role was to oversee the planning and execution of Operation Overlord, the largest amphibious invasion in history, which aimed to establish a foothold in Nazi-occupied Western Europe. Known as D-Day, the invasion was launched on June 6, 1944, with Eisenhower at the helm.

Eisenhower's leadership qualities shone brightly during the challenging planning stages of D-Day. He demonstrated remarkable diplomatic skills in managing the diverse group of Allied leaders and commanders from the United States, Britain, Canada, and other nations. His ability to mediate differing opinions and forge a united front was crucial to the success of the operation.

On D-Day, Eisenhower's responsibility extended beyond military strategy. He faced the immense task of coordinating land, sea, and air forces, ensuring that the invasion was executed with precision. Despite the risks and uncertainties, Eisenhower's calm and steady demeanor inspired confidence in his subordinates and troops. His famous "Eisenhower Jacket" became a symbol of his approachable leadership style.

The success of the Normandy landings marked a turning point in the war. Eisenhower's leadership enabled the Allies to establish a beachhead in France, leading to the liberation of Western Europe from Nazi control. From that point on, Eisenhower directed Allied forces in a series of offensives, including the Battle of the Bulge and the eventual defeat of Nazi Germany.

Eisenhower's role extended beyond the battlefield. As the Allied forces advanced, he recognized the importance of working with local populations to restore stability and rebuild nations devastated by war. His emphasis on minimizing civilian casualties and fostering goodwill contributed to the successful occupation and reconstruction of Europe.

One of Eisenhower's most significant contributions came after the war. As Allied forces approached victory, he played a key role in the unconditional surrender of Germany. His leadership qualities were again evident in navigating the delicate negotiations with Soviet leaders, helping to lay the groundwork for the post-war world order.

After World War II, Eisenhower's leadership continued to shape history. He served as the Supreme Commander of the North Atlantic Treaty Organization (NATO), working to strengthen the collective defense of Western nations against the threat of Soviet expansion. In 1952, he was elected as the 34th President of the United States, bringing his leadership qualities to the realm of domestic and international politics.

In conclusion, General Dwight D. Eisenhower's role in World War II was marked by his exceptional leadership, strategic brilliance, and ability to unite diverse Allied forces.

General George Patton

General George S. Patton, a charismatic and bold military leader, played a distinctive role in World War II as one of the most iconic and dynamic commanders. Known for his aggressive tactics, unwavering determination, and legendary leadership, Patton left an indelible mark on the course of the war and the outcome of pivotal battles.

Patton's leadership journey during World War II began in North Africa, where he commanded the U.S. II Corps during Operation Torch in November 1942. His strategic brilliance and aggressive style of warfare contributed to the success of this initial Allied campaign, which aimed to oust Axis forces from North Africa. Patton's audacious and rapid advances earned him the nickname "Old Blood and Guts."

One of Patton's most remarkable accomplishments came during the pivotal Battle of Sicily in 1943. Tasked with leading the U.S. Seventh Army, Patton executed a daring amphibious assault, quickly gaining a foothold on the island. His tactical acumen and swift maneuvering led to the liberation of Sicily from Axis control. This triumph showcased his ability to inspire his troops and achieve significant objectives.

The breakout from Normandy following the D-Day landings marked another critical phase of Patton's role in the war. As the commander of the U.S. Third Army, he demonstrated his exceptional leadership by spearheading a rapid and relentless advance across France. His audacious tactics and ability to exploit enemy weaknesses facilitated the liberation of key French cities and contributed to the disruption of German defenses.

The Battle of the Bulge, a pivotal moment in the war, showcased Patton's tenacity and strategic brilliance. When the German forces launched a surprise counteroffensive in the Ardennes forest, Patton's Third Army played a crucial role in relieving the besieged town of Bastogne. His swift response and aggressive approach helped thwart the German advance and turn the tide in favor of the Allies.

Patton's dynamic leadership style extended beyond the battlefield. His distinctive charisma and unapologetic commitment to victory resonated deeply with his troops. His famous speeches, motivating rallies, and unconventional practices, such as donning flashy uniforms and owning a pair of ivory-handled revolvers, further established his legendary status.

However, Patton's career was not without controversies. His outspoken nature and sometimes abrasive comments led to conflicts with higher command and political leaders. In 1943, he was temporarily relieved of command after making derogatory remarks about soldiers suffering from battle fatigue. Despite these setbacks, Patton's military prowess and undeniable impact on the outcome of battles remained undeniable.

In conclusion, General George S. Patton's role in World War II was characterized by his dynamic leadership, aggressive tactics, and significant accomplishments in key battles. From North Africa to Sicily, Normandy, and the Ardennes, Patton's audacity and strategic brilliance played a pivotal role in the Allied victory.

General Erwin Rommel

General Erwin Rommel, often referred to as the "Desert Fox," was a prominent figure in World War II, known for his strategic brilliance and leadership in the North African campaign. As a German military commander, Rommel played a significant role in key battles and left a lasting impact on the war's history.

Rommel's most notable achievements occurred in the North African theater of the war. He led the German and Italian forces in a series of successful campaigns against the Allied forces, earning him a reputation as a skilled tactician. His early victories in North Africa, particularly the capture of Tobruk in 1942, showcased his ability to outmaneuver his opponents and exploit weaknesses in their defenses.

Rommel's dynamic leadership style and innovative tactics earned him the nickname "Desert Fox." He was known for his daring and rapid movements across the desert, often catching his adversaries off guard. His ability to inspire his troops and lead from the frontlines made him a respected figure among his soldiers.

However, Rommel's successes were not without setbacks. The Battle of El Alamein in 1942 marked a turning point in the North African campaign. Despite his tactical skills, Rommel faced defeat at the hands of the British under General Bernard Montgomery. The battle halted his advance and marked the beginning of a retreat for Axis forces in the region.

Rommel's role extended beyond North Africa. He was tasked with overseeing the defenses along the Atlantic Wall in preparation for a possible Allied invasion of Western Europe. His efforts in fortifying coastal defenses showcased his dedication to his duties, even in the face of challenging circumstances.

One of Rommel's most controversial actions was his involvement in a plot to assassinate Adolf Hitler. He became disillusioned with Hitler's leadership and the direction of the war. However, the assassination attempt failed, and Rommel was implicated in the conspiracy. He was given the option to take his own life or face a trial. In 1944, he chose to take his life to protect his family.

In conclusion, General Erwin Rommel played a significant role in World War II, particularly in the North African campaign. His strategic brilliance and innovative tactics led to notable victories, but he also faced defeats, such as at El Alamein.

General Charles de Gaulle

Charles de Gaulle played a pivotal role in World War II as a prominent French military leader and statesman. Born on November 22, 1890, in Lille, France, de Gaulle's contributions during the war significantly impacted the course of history. As a middle school social studies teacher, you can use this simplified description to help your students understand his role at a 500 Lexile level.

At the outset of World War II, Germany's invasion of France in 1940 led to a swift defeat for the French forces. During this challenging time, Charles de Gaulle emerged as a voice of resilience and hope for the French people. He believed that France should continue fighting against the German occupation rather than accepting defeat.

De Gaulle's most notable moment came on June 18, 1940, when he delivered a radio broadcast from London. In this stirring speech, he called on the French to resist the German occupation and continue the fight for their country's freedom. He famously declared, "France has lost a battle, but France has not lost the war."

Establishing himself as the leader of the Free French Forces, de Gaulle worked to gather support from other French colonies and territories around the world. He aimed to create a united front against the Axis powers, including Germany and Italy. Under his leadership, the Free French Forces participated in important military campaigns, such as the liberation of North Africa.

De Gaulle's relationship with the Allied powers, particularly the United Kingdom and the United States, was sometimes complex. He sought to ensure that France had a prominent role in the post-war world and that its interests were considered alongside those of the other Allies. This led to negotiations and discussions that shaped the post-war landscape.

One of the significant moments of de Gaulle's involvement in World War II was his leadership during the Normandy landings in 1944. As Allied forces stormed the beaches of Normandy to liberate France from German control, de Gaulle's presence and support boosted the morale of both the French people and the Allied troops. His participation in the liberation of Paris later that year further solidified his position as a symbol of French resistance and determination.

After the war, Charles de Gaulle played a crucial role in the reconstruction of France. He became the President of the French Provisional Government and worked to establish a new constitution for the country. In 1958, he returned to power as the President of the Fifth Republic, a position he held until 1969.

De Gaulle's legacy in World War II remains that of a steadfast leader who refused to accept defeat and rallied his countrymen to continue fighting. His determination and courage inspired not only the French people but also people around the world who were yearning for freedom and justice. His role in shaping the post-war world and his contributions to the strengthening of France's position on the global stage are remembered as enduring accomplishments.

Audie Murphy

Audie Murphy, an American hero of World War II, is widely celebrated for his extraordinary bravery and valor on the battlefield. Born on June 20, 1925, in Kingston, Texas, Murphy grew up in poverty and faced numerous challenges before enlisting in the U.S. Army in 1942, at the young age of 17.

During World War II, Murphy served with the 3rd Infantry Division and saw action in North Africa, Sicily, Italy, and France. He quickly earned a reputation for his courage and determination in the face of danger. One of his most famous acts of bravery occurred on January 26, 1945, in Holtzwihr, France, during the Battle of the Colmar Pocket. As his company was pinned down by heavy German machine gun fire, Murphy single-handedly took on the enemy, killing several German soldiers and silencing the machine gun with grenades. Despite being wounded in the leg, he continued to lead his men and eventually repelled the German counterattack.

For his exceptional bravery during the battle, Audie Murphy was awarded the Medal of Honor, the highest military decoration in the United States. He became one of the most decorated soldiers of World War II, earning a total of 33 awards and medals, including the Distinguished Service Cross, two Silver Stars, three Purple Hearts, and the French Legion of Honor.

Beyond his heroics on the battlefield, Audie Murphy also showcased his leadership and tactical skills during his military service. He was promoted to the rank of second lieutenant and served as a platoon leader, earning the respect and admiration of his fellow soldiers.

After the war, Audie Murphy's experiences haunted him, leading to struggles with post-traumatic stress disorder (PTSD). Despite the challenges he faced, he channeled his pain into advocacy for the recognition of PTSD and mental health issues faced by veterans. He used his fame to raise awareness and help veterans receive the support they needed.

In addition to his military achievements, Audie Murphy had a successful career as an actor and appeared in over 40 films, including the autobiographical movie "To Hell and Back," based on his wartime experiences.

Tragically, on May 28, 1971, Audie Murphy's life came to a premature end when he died in a plane crash at the age of 45. His passing was a profound loss to the nation and the military community.

Audie Murphy's legacy as a brave and selfless soldier continues to inspire generations of Americans. His indomitable spirit and unwavering commitment to duty serve as a reminder of the sacrifices made by all those who have served their country in times of war. Audie Murphy remains an enduring symbol of courage, resilience, and the profound impact one individual can have on history.

Richard "Dick" Best

Richard "Dick" Best was a remarkable figure whose bravery and skill left an indelible mark on World War II. His role in the war showcased his unwavering dedication to duty, making him a true hero of his time.

Born on March 24, 1910, in California, Dick Best grew up with a deep fascination for aviation. His dreams took flight when he joined the United States Navy, where he eventually became a dive-bomber pilot. Little did he know that his actions would shape the course of history.

Best's most significant contributions came during the Battle of Midway, a critical conflict that took place in the Pacific Ocean in June 1942. This battle marked a turning point in the war, with the aircraft carrier USS Yorktown and its pilots playing a pivotal role. As a member of the Yorktown's air group, Best's skills were put to the test.

During the battle, Best's leadership and determination shone through. On June 4, 1942, he led a daring dive-bombing attack on the Japanese aircraft carrier Akagi, a key vessel in the Japanese fleet. Despite facing intense anti-aircraft fire and enemy fighter planes, Best remained undeterred. His precision in dropping bombs directly onto the Akagi's deck dealt a crippling blow to the Japanese forces.

Best's heroic actions did not stop there. On the same day, he targeted the Japanese carrier Hiryu. With his exceptional marksmanship, he managed to disable the Hiryu, leaving it vulnerable to subsequent attacks. His fearless and calculated decisions were crucial in weakening Japan's naval strength during the battle.

Dick Best's contributions extended beyond his strategic prowess. His leadership and ability to stay composed under pressure inspired his fellow pilots. Despite the chaos of battle, Best's presence served as a beacon of courage and determination, urging his comrades to follow his lead.

The Battle of Midway's significance cannot be overstated. The United States' victory in this conflict turned the tide of the war in the Pacific and halted Japan's expansion. Dick Best's actions played an integral role in achieving this victory. His precise bombing runs not only crippled enemy carriers but also showcased the importance of skilled pilots in naval warfare.

His legacy lives on as a testament to the heroes of World War II and the sacrifices they made to ensure a safer world.

Wade McClusky

Wade McClusky was a remarkable figure whose strategic decisions and leadership had a significant impact during World War II. As a United States Navy officer, he played a crucial role in the pivotal Battle of Midway, a turning point in the Pacific Theater of the war.

Born on January 12, 1902, in Buffalo, New York, Wade McClusky joined the U.S. Naval Academy and graduated in 1926. He began his naval career as a pilot, becoming skilled in operating carrier-based aircraft. His experience and expertise would later prove invaluable in the heat of battle.

One of McClusky's most notable contributions occurred during the Battle of Midway in June 1942. At this critical juncture, the United States and Japan were locked in a fierce struggle for control over the Pacific. The Japanese aimed to eliminate American aircraft carriers and secure dominance in the region.

During the battle, McClusky was a commander of the USS Enterprise's air group. On June 4, 1942, he led a dive-bombing squadron of Douglas SBD Dauntless dive-bombers on a daring search mission. While other pilots had difficulty finding the Japanese fleet, McClusky's keen instincts and sharp decision-making led him to spot the Japanese carriers.

Despite facing challenging weather conditions and low fuel, McClusky's squadron persevered and managed to locate the Japanese carrier Kaga. His accurate determination of the enemy's position and the subsequent attack on Kaga contributed to the carrier's destruction. This action, along with the coordinated efforts of other American forces, played a pivotal role in turning the tide of the battle.

The destruction of Kaga, along with three other Japanese carriers, marked a significant turning point in the Pacific Theater. The Battle of Midway crippled Japan's carrier fleet and curtailed its expansion in the Pacific. McClusky's leadership, courage, and decision-making were instrumental in securing this crucial victory.

Wade McClusky's strategic prowess didn't end with the Battle of Midway. He continued to serve in various roles, contributing to the success of subsequent campaigns in the Pacific. His dedication to duty and outstanding leadership earned him respect among his peers and superiors.

McClusky retired from the Navy in 1956 as a rear admiral. His contributions during World War II and his impact on the outcome of the Battle of Midway solidified his legacy as a key figure in naval history. His ability to make critical decisions under pressure, his determination to locate the enemy carriers, and his willingness to take risks were essential elements that influenced the course of the war.

Wade McClusky's story serves as a testament to the importance of leadership, determination, and strategic thinking in times of conflict. His actions during the Battle of Midway demonstrated how individual decisions can shape the outcomes of significant events and alter the course of history.

Heinrich Himmler

Heinrich Himmler was a key figure in Nazi Germany, serving as the chief architect of the SS (Schutzstaffel) and one of the principal architects of the Holocaust. Born on October 7, 1900, in Munich, Germany, Himmler played a crucial role in shaping the structure of the Nazi regime and implementing its brutal policies.

In the early years of his life, Himmler displayed an interest in nationalist and militaristic ideologies. He joined the Nazi Party in 1923 and participated in the failed Beer Hall Putsch, a coup attempt led by Adolf Hitler. Despite the failure, Himmler remained dedicated to the Nazi cause and rose through the ranks due to his organizational skills and unwavering loyalty.

Himmler's significant influence began in 1929 when he became the head of the SS, a paramilitary organization initially formed as Hitler's personal bodyguard. Under Himmler's leadership, the SS evolved into a formidable force with immense power, controlling various aspects of the Nazi state, including the secret police and concentration camps.

One of Himmler's most infamous roles was overseeing the implementation of the Final Solution, the systematic genocide of six million Jews during the Holocaust. He played a central role in planning and executing the genocide, coordinating the mass murder of innocent people in concentration and extermination camps. Himmler's chilling efficiency in organizing the logistics of mass extermination is a dark chapter in human history.

Apart from his involvement in the Holocaust, Himmler was instrumental in shaping the racial policies of Nazi Germany. He promoted the concept of Aryan racial purity and actively pursued eugenics programs to eliminate perceived "racial impurities." His policies led to the forced sterilization and euthanasia of individuals with disabilities, as well as the persecution of various ethnic and religious groups.

Himmler's influence extended beyond the military and political realms. He played a crucial role in the indoctrination of Nazi ideology among the German youth through the Hitler Youth and the education system. Himmler sought to create a generation of loyal followers who would perpetuate the Nazi worldview.

In the later stages of World War II, as Germany faced defeat, Himmler attempted to negotiate with the Allies to secure a separate peace. However, his efforts were in vain, and as the Allies closed in, he attempted to evade capture. Himmler was eventually captured by British forces in May 1945. Realizing the gravity of his crimes, he committed suicide through cyanide poisoning before he could face justice at the Nuremberg Trials.

Heinrich Himmler's legacy is one of infamy, representing the darkest aspects of Nazi ideology and its implementation. His role in orchestrating the genocide of millions and promoting racist doctrines makes him a symbol of the atrocities committed during the Holocaust. The name Heinrich Himmler remains synonymous with the horrors of the Nazi regime and serves as a stark reminder of the consequences of unchecked extremism and hatred.

Josef Goebbels

Josef Goebbels, born on October 29, 1897, in Rheydt, Germany, was a prominent figure in Nazi Germany and Adolf Hitler's Minister of Propaganda. Known for his exceptional oratory skills and propaganda expertise, Goebbels played a crucial role in shaping public opinion to align with the Nazi ideology during the 1930s and 1940s.

Goebbels initially studied at the University of Heidelberg, where he earned a Ph.D. in philosophy. However, his aspirations in academia took a back seat when he joined the Nazi Party in 1924, just a year after its formation. His fervent dedication to the party and Hitler's vision propelled him into positions of increasing influence.

As Minister of Propaganda, Goebbels had a significant impact on the dissemination of information and the manipulation of public sentiment. He recognized the power of media and used it effectively to spread Nazi propaganda, control narratives, and consolidate support for the regime. Goebbels skillfully utilized newspapers, radio broadcasts, and other forms of media to influence public opinion, employing techniques that would later become infamous for their manipulation and distortion of reality.

One of Goebbels' most infamous achievements was his orchestration of the infamous book burnings that took place on May 10, 1933. Targeting books deemed "un-German" or contrary to Nazi ideology, the burning symbolized the suppression of dissenting voices and the establishment of Nazi cultural dominance. Goebbels saw the event as a powerful tool to shape the narrative and control intellectual discourse within Germany.

Goebbels was also instrumental in the production of propaganda films, recognizing their potential to convey ideological messages effectively. Films like "Triumph of the Will" directed by Leni Riefenstahl and "The Eternal Jew" aimed to glorify the Nazi regime and demonize perceived enemies, employing cinematic techniques to manipulate emotions and perceptions.

As a loyal supporter of Hitler, Goebbels became increasingly influential within the Nazi hierarchy. His unwavering loyalty earned him Hitler's trust, and he was appointed Reichsminister in 1933, overseeing the Ministry of Propaganda and Public Enlightenment. In this role, Goebbels had the authority to shape cultural and intellectual life in Nazi Germany.

Despite his prominence in the Nazi regime, Goebbels faced personal challenges. His wife, Magda, was of partial Jewish descent, which led to considerable internal conflict. However, Goebbels' loyalty to Hitler and the Nazi cause remained steadfast, and he went to great lengths to conceal this fact.

As World War II unfolded, Goebbels intensified his efforts to maintain morale on the home front through propaganda. However, as the war took a turn for the worse for the Nazis, Goebbels' propaganda machine faced greater challenges in presenting a positive image to the German public. In the final days of the war, with defeat imminent, Goebbels and his wife committed suicide in the garden of the Reich Chancellery on May 1, 1945.

Josef Goebbels' legacy remains one of manipulation, deceit, and the ruthless use of propaganda to further a destructive ideology. His role in shaping public opinion during a dark chapter in history serves as a stark reminder of the power of media and the dangers of unchecked propaganda.

Josef Mengele

Josef Mengele, born on March 16, 1911, in Günzburg, Germany, was a notorious figure in the history of the Holocaust. Often referred to as the "Angel of Death," Mengele was a German SS officer and physician who gained infamy for his inhumane experiments on inmates at Auschwitz concentration camp during World War II.

Mengele received his medical degree from the University of Frankfurt in 1935 and later joined the Nazi Party in 1937. As a member of the SS, he became deeply entrenched in the racist and anti-Semitic ideology of the Nazi regime. His involvement with the Auschwitz concentration camp began in 1943, where he was assigned to the medical staff.

One of Mengele's most horrifying legacies is his role in conducting gruesome medical experiments on prisoners, particularly twins. He was fascinated by the genetic aspect of heredity and sought to explore it through his sadistic experiments. Twins, children, and individuals with physical abnormalities were subjected to torturous procedures without their consent, including sterilization, surgeries, injections, and exposure to lethal substances. These experiments caused immense suffering and led to the deaths of numerous innocent victims.

Mengele's obsession with twins stemmed from his desire to unlock supposed genetic secrets that would contribute to the Nazi ideology of racial purity. His actions were a manifestation of the warped beliefs that underpinned the Holocaust, where individuals were dehumanized and subjected to unspeakable horrors in the name of pseudo-scientific research.

While Mengele's sadistic experiments were a defining aspect of his time at Auschwitz, he was also involved in the selection process upon the arrival of new prisoners. Standing on the platform as trains arrived, he would determine who would be sent to the gas chambers for immediate extermination and who would be subjected to forced labor or his experiments.

This role in the selection process further solidified his reputation as the "Angel of Death."

As Allied forces advanced towards the end of World War II, Mengele fled Auschwitz in January 1945. He managed to evade capture and lived in various locations, including South America. Mengele's ability to escape justice for his heinous crimes haunted survivors and those seeking accountability for the Holocaust.

It wasn't until 1985 that forensic experts confirmed Mengele's death through drowning in Brazil in 1979. His remains were exhumed, and DNA testing confirmed his identity. The lack of justice for Mengele fueled ongoing debates about the effectiveness of post-war efforts to hold war criminals accountable for their actions.

Josef Mengele's legacy remains an indelible stain on human history, symbolizing the depths of cruelty that individuals can descend to under the influence of extremist ideologies. His actions at Auschwitz epitomize the dehumanization and brutality that characterized the Holocaust, serving as a stark reminder of the atrocities committed during one of the darkest chapters in modern history. The quest for justice and remembrance of the victims continue to be integral in preventing the recurrence of such horrors and upholding the principles of humanity and compassion.

African Americans in World War II

In World War II, African Americans played a vital role on the battlefield, demonstrating remarkable courage and resilience in the face of discrimination and adversity. Despite facing segregation and racial prejudice within the military, African American soldiers served with distinction in various units, making significant contributions to the Allied victory.

One of the most well-known African American units in World War II was the Tuskegee Airmen. These skilled fighter pilots, trained at the Tuskegee Army Air Field in Alabama, became the first African American military aviators in the United States Armed Forces. The Tuskegee Airmen were tasked with escorting bombers on dangerous missions over Europe, facing enemy fire and defending against Luftwaffe attacks. Their exceptional performance earned them a reputation as skilled and reliable aviators, proving the capabilities of African American soldiers and breaking down racial barriers within the military.

Another remarkable African American unit was the 761st Tank Battalion, known as the "Black Panthers." This tank battalion was composed of skilled tankers who demonstrated great bravery and proficiency in combat. They played a crucial role in the liberation of towns and cities in Europe, often facing heavy resistance from German forces. Despite the challenges of racism and prejudice, the 761st Tank Battalion earned numerous commendations for their gallantry in battle.

In Italy, the 92nd Infantry Division, nicknamed the "Buffalo Soldiers," fought tenaciously to advance against formidable German defenses. The Buffalo Soldiers faced not only enemy fire but also racial discrimination within the military. Despite these hardships, they displayed unwavering determination and bravery, making significant contributions to the Allied effort in Italy.

Beyond the battlefield, African Americans also contributed to the war effort on the home front. Many worked in defense industries, producing crucial war materials, aircraft, and ships. Their efforts were instrumental in supporting the war effort and supplying the troops overseas.

Despite their sacrifices and achievements, African American soldiers faced racial segregation and discrimination within the military. They were often assigned to segregated units, denied access to certain facilities, and excluded from leadership roles. However, their bravery and dedication challenged prevailing racial attitudes, eventually leading to the desegregation of the armed forces through President Harry S. Truman's Executive Order 9981 in 1948.

The contributions of African Americans in World War II were not limited to military service. African American women played essential roles as nurses, clerks, and support personnel, contributing to the war effort both at home and overseas.

The legacy of African Americans in World War II remains a powerful testament to their determination and patriotism. Their bravery and sacrifices paved the way for increased civil rights and equality in the United States. Their service and heroism continue to be celebrated, honoring the indelible impact they had on the nation's history and the fight for justice and equality.

Daniel "Chappie" James

Daniel "Chappie" James, a pioneering figure in the United States Air Force, rose to prominence as a skilled aviator and military leader, breaking barriers and paving the way for future generations of African American military personnel. Born on February 11, 1920, in Pensacola, Florida, James' journey was marked by remarkable achievements and a commitment to excellence.

Chappie James entered the world of aviation at a time when racial segregation was prevalent in the military. Despite facing systemic challenges and discrimination, he excelled as a pilot. In 1943, James completed his pilot training at Tuskegee Army Airfield, part of the Tuskegee Airmen program—an initiative aimed at training African American pilots during World War II.

His skill and determination earned him a place among the elite pilots of the 332nd Fighter Group, known as the "Red Tails." James distinguished himself as a fighter pilot, flying numerous combat missions over Europe during the war. His courageous and skilled performance in the air earned him the respect of his peers and superiors.

Following World War II, Chappie James continued to break barriers in the military. In 1947, when the United States Air Force became a separate branch of the military, he remained a part of this new and independent force. Over the next decades, he rose through the ranks, achieving the rank of brigadier general in 1966, making him the first African American to attain the rank in the U.S. Air Force.

Chappie James' leadership skills were put to the test during the Vietnam War, where he served as the vice commander of the 8th Tactical Fighter Wing. He flew combat missions over North Vietnam, showcasing not only his bravery but also his commitment to leading from the front. His exceptional performance led to numerous accolades, and in 1970, he became the first African American to achieve the rank of four-star general in the U.S. military.

General Daniel "Chappie" James assumed command of the North American Aerospace Defense Command (NORAD) in 1975, further solidifying his place in history. His appointment to such a high-ranking position marked a significant milestone in the integration of African Americans into leadership roles within the military.

Chappie James' legacy extends beyond his military achievements. He became an influential advocate for equal opportunities and diversity within the armed forces. His charisma, coupled with a steadfast commitment to excellence, inspired countless individuals to pursue careers in aviation and the military, irrespective of their background.

Throughout his career, General James faced the dual challenges of proving himself in the predominantly white world of military aviation and advocating for equal opportunities for African Americans. His achievements, marked by professionalism and a commitment to service, helped dismantle racial barriers within the U.S. military.

Chappie James retired from the Air Force in 1978, leaving behind a legacy that continues to inspire. He passed away on February 25, 1978, but his impact lives on in the achievements of those who followed in his footsteps. The Daniel "Chappie" James Jr. Center for Aerospace Science and Health Education was established in his honor, ensuring that his story and contributions are remembered for generations to come.

In commemorating Daniel "Chappie" James, we acknowledge not only his individual accomplishments but also the broader significance of his role in breaking racial barriers, advocating for equality, and shaping the landscape of the U.S. military. His legacy remains a testament to the power of perseverance and excellence in the face of adversity.

Dorie Miller

Dorie Miller, a remarkable figure in World War II, played a significant role that defied racial barriers and inspired generations. Born on October 12, 1919, in Waco, Texas, Miller enlisted in the United States Navy in 1939, serving as a mess attendant, a job typically assigned to African American sailors during that time.

On December 7, 1941, the Japanese launched a surprise attack on the U.S. naval base at Pearl Harbor, Hawaii, plunging the United States into World War II. During the chaos of the attack on the USS West Virginia, Miller's bravery and heroism came to the forefront. Despite his assigned duties as a mess attendant, he immediately responded to the call of duty when he saw that the ship's anti-aircraft guns were under attack.

Ignoring the fact that he had not received formal training as a gunner, Miller manned one of the anti-aircraft machine guns with incredible courage. Despite the overwhelming odds, he managed to shoot down several enemy aircraft, displaying exceptional marksmanship and bravery. His actions earned him praise from his fellow sailors and officers, who later commended his gallantry in the face of danger.

Dorie Miller's heroism did not go unnoticed by the media and the American public. His actions were widely reported, making him a symbol of courage and resilience during a time of great national uncertainty. In 1942, the Navy awarded him the Navy Cross, making him the first African American to receive this prestigious honor during World War II.

Miller's actions had a profound impact on the fight for civil rights in the United States. At a time when African Americans faced discrimination and segregation, his valor and recognition challenged prevailing racial attitudes and helped pave the way for increased opportunities for African Americans in the military.

Following the events at Pearl Harbor, Miller continued to serve in the Navy and participated in the Pacific theater of the war. Tragically, on November 24, 1943, while aboard the USS Liscome Bay during the Battle of Makin Island, the ship was struck by a Japanese torpedo and sank. Dorie Miller was among the hundreds of sailors who lost their lives in the tragic incident.

In the years following his death, Miller's legacy lived on as a symbol of courage and determination in the face of adversity. His heroism inspired African Americans to continue pushing for civil rights and equal opportunities in the armed forces. In 1973, the Navy commissioned the USS Miller, a Knox-class frigate, in his honor.

Dorie Miller's story remains an enduring testament to the contributions of African Americans to the nation's defense and their ability to overcome obstacles in the pursuit of justice and equality. His bravery in the face of discrimination and his heroism during the attack on Pearl Harbor made him a true American hero, and his legacy continues to inspire and empower generations.

761st Tank Battalion

The 761st Tank Battalion, an African American unit, played a significant and historic role in both World War II and the civil rights movement in the United States. Known as the "Black Panthers," this pioneering tank battalion defied racial barriers and demonstrated exceptional valor on the battlefield.

During World War II, African Americans faced systemic discrimination and segregation within the US military. The prevailing belief was that they lacked the ability to effectively serve in combat roles. However, the pressing need for manpower led to the formation of the 761st Tank Battalion in early 1942. Despite initial skepticism, this unit proved their capabilities during rigorous training and was deployed to the European Theater of Operations.

The 761st Tank Battalion faced immense challenges and racial prejudice while serving in Europe. They were often assigned to support other units and faced limited opportunities for direct combat. However, their tenacity and dedication to duty eventually earned them a chance to prove their mettle in battle.

In November 1944, the 761st Tank Battalion saw its first taste of combat in the Battle of the Bulge. During this crucial engagement, they played a critical role in countering the German offensive, breaking through enemy lines, and rescuing the "Lost Battalion" - a group of trapped American soldiers. The unit's exceptional performance under fire garnered praise from their fellow soldiers and higher-ranking officers.

As the war continued, the 761st Tank Battalion participated in several other significant campaigns, including the Rhineland and Central Europe campaigns. Their bravery and combat prowess helped secure crucial victories for the Allies. Despite their exceptional service, the unit faced continued racial segregation and discrimination, both within the military and on the home front.

Upon returning to the United States after the war, the members of the 761st Tank Battalion were hailed as heroes, but their efforts to improve civil rights for African Americans did not end on the battlefield. They had experienced firsthand the injustices of segregation, both within the military and in their communities.

Many veterans of the 761st Tank Battalion became advocates for civil rights, using their military service as a platform to demand equality and social justice. Their activism and leadership were crucial in laying the foundation for the civil rights movement that would gain momentum in the coming years.

The legacy of the 761st Tank Battalion and its contributions to the civil rights movement cannot be overstated. Their courage and sacrifice on the battlefield served as a powerful counterargument to the prevailing racist beliefs about African Americans' abilities. The unit's success paved the way for the integration of the US military, which President Harry S. Truman officially ordered in 1948.

The 761st Tank Battalion's remarkable achievements and their subsequent involvement in the civil rights movement set a precedent for future generations of African Americans seeking to break barriers and fight for equality. Their journey from being marginalized and underestimated to becoming celebrated heroes and advocates serves as an enduring testament to the power of determination, courage, and perseverance in the face of adversity. The "Black Panthers" left an indelible mark on American history, both as valiant soldiers during World War II and as trailblazers in the ongoing fight for civil rights and social justice.

92nd Infantry Division

The 92nd Infantry Division, also known as the "Buffalo Soldiers," played a crucial role in World War II, making significant contributions to the Allied effort in Italy. Composed primarily of African American soldiers, the division faced not only enemy fire but also racial discrimination and segregation within the military. Despite these challenges, the Buffalo Soldiers displayed unwavering determination, bravery, and valor throughout the war.

Formed in October 1942, the 92nd Infantry Division was one of the few African American divisions in the U.S. Army at the time. Their nickname, "Buffalo Soldiers," harkened back to the famed African American cavalry units that served in the American West after the Civil War. This name was proudly embraced by the soldiers of the division, symbolizing their heritage and warrior spirit.

The division's first major engagement occurred during the Italian Campaign, where they were assigned to the Fifth Army under General Mark W. Clark. The Buffalo Soldiers faced daunting challenges as they fought against the well-fortified German defenses, rugged terrain, and harsh weather conditions.

Despite the harsh circumstances, the 92nd Infantry Division demonstrated exceptional combat skills and bravery, earning the respect of their fellow soldiers and commanders. They played a significant role in key battles, including the Battle of Anzio and the liberation of the city of Bologna.

One of the division's most remarkable achievements was during the Battle of Montecassino. In May 1944, the Buffalo Soldiers were part of the Allied assault on the well-fortified Monte Cassino Abbey, which was occupied by German forces. The fierce and determined fighting by the 92nd Infantry Division helped secure the strategic abbey and paved the way for the Allied advance.

Throughout the Italian Campaign, the Buffalo Soldiers faced not only enemy fire but also racial discrimination and segregation within the military. They were often assigned to menial tasks and support roles, while white units were given more prominent combat assignments. Despite these obstacles, the division's soldiers exhibited extraordinary resilience and determination, proving their capabilities as skilled and valiant fighters.

By the end of the war, the 92nd Infantry Division had earned a reputation for their tenacity, bravery, and contributions to the Allied victory in Italy. Their unwavering commitment to their duty and fellow soldiers set a remarkable example of courage and fortitude.

After World War II, the legacy of the 92nd Infantry Division continued to inspire African Americans in their fight for civil rights and equality in the United States. The Buffalo Soldiers' heroism and sacrifices played a significant role in challenging racial prejudices within the military and the broader society.

Today, the 92nd Infantry Division's contributions are remembered and honored as a testament to the bravery and dedication of African American soldiers in World War II. The Buffalo Soldiers' role in the Italian Campaign stands as a symbol of the indomitable spirit of the African American troops who served their country with honor and valor despite facing discrimination and adversity.

Tuskegee Airmen

The Tuskegee Airmen were a group of remarkable African American pilots and support personnel who shattered racial barriers during World War II. These brave men demonstrated unwavering courage, determination, and exceptional skills as aviators, leaving an indelible mark on American military history.

At a time when racial segregation prevailed in the United States military, African Americans were largely denied opportunities for combat roles. In 1941, the U.S. Army Air Corps initiated an experimental program aimed at training African American pilots at the Tuskegee Institute in Tuskegee, Alabama. This program, known as the Tuskegee Experience, sought to challenge prejudices and prove the capabilities of African American servicemen.

Undergoing rigorous training at Moton Field in Tuskegee, the aspiring aviators mastered the art of aerial combat and flying maneuvers. Despite facing racial discrimination and skepticism about their abilities, the Tuskegee Airmen persevered, proving themselves as highly skilled aviators. They earned their wings and officer commissions, displaying a level of expertise that defied the prevailing racial biases of the time.

In 1943, the Tuskegee Airmen formed the 332nd Fighter Group and the 477th Bombardment Group, becoming the first African American military aviators in U.S. history. Their primary mission was to provide escort protection for American bombers flying over Europe during World War II.

One of the most remarkable achievements of the Tuskegee Airmen was their astounding record of never losing a single bomber to enemy aircraft during their escort missions. The 332nd Fighter Group, in particular, gained widespread recognition for their exceptional performance, leading to the moniker "Red Tails" due to the distinctive red paint on the tails of their aircraft.

Their success in safeguarding bombers not only demonstrated their extraordinary skills but also helped dispel prevailing doubts about African American abilities in aviation. The Tuskegee Airmen's accomplishments played a pivotal role in dismantling racial prejudices within the military and paved the way for the eventual desegregation of the U.S. armed forces in 1948.

Beyond their combat achievements, the Tuskegee Airmen became symbols of hope and resilience for African Americans across the nation. Their determination to excel in the face of adversity and racial discrimination inspired countless individuals to challenge systemic racism and advocate for civil rights.

However, even after the war, the Tuskegee Airmen continued to face discrimination and unequal treatment. Nevertheless, their legacy endured and continued to influence the civil rights movement in the ensuing decades.

In recognition of their valor and dedication during World War II, the Tuskegee Airmen were collectively awarded the Congressional Gold Medal in 2007, the highest civilian honor in the United States. This prestigious award served as a belated acknowledgment of their bravery and marked a significant step in the nation's efforts to confront its historical racial injustices.

The 1st Special Service Force in World War II

The 1st Special Service Force, also known as the "Devil's Brigade," was a unique and elite American-Canadian commando unit that played a crucial role in World War II. Formed in 1942, this joint venture between the United States and Canada brought together highly trained soldiers with diverse skills, creating a force that excelled in unconventional and specialized operations.

The unit's creation stemmed from the need for a specialized force capable of conducting high-risk and challenging missions in the harsh terrains of the European theater. The 1st Special Service Force was a blend of American and Canadian soldiers, with a reputation for being exceptionally skilled and physically fit. Their distinctive training set them apart, combining elements of commando, airborne, and mountain warfare tactics.

The Devil's Brigade earned its nickname through a combination of the soldiers' unique training and the insignia they wore – a spearhead with an arrowhead in the center, symbolizing the force's ability to penetrate enemy lines. Their training included hand-to-hand combat, stealth operations, parachuting, and winter warfare tactics, making them a versatile and formidable unit.

One of the defining characteristics of the Devil's Brigade was its proficiency in mountain warfare. This expertise became particularly valuable during the Allied campaigns in Italy, where the rugged and mountainous terrain posed significant challenges. The force's ability to navigate and fight in such conditions gave them a strategic advantage, allowing them to carry out successful raids and sabotage missions against Axis forces.

One of the most notable operations conducted by the 1st Special Service Force was the assault on Monte La Difensa in December 1943. Perched atop a steep mountain, the German stronghold presented a formidable obstacle. The Devil's

Brigade executed a daring nighttime assault, climbing the treacherous slopes and surprising the enemy with their exceptional mountaineering skills. The success of this mission showcased the unit's unique capabilities and solidified its reputation as an elite force.

Beyond their prowess in mountainous environments, the Devil's Brigade was also trained for amphibious operations. They participated in the Allied landings at Anzio, Italy, in 1944, where their amphibious and commando skills were put to the test. The unit faced intense fighting as they pushed inland, demonstrating their adaptability in different combat scenarios.

The 1st Special Service Force's contributions extended beyond the European theater. After the success in Italy, the unit was deployed to southern France and later participated in the liberation of the French town of Menton. Their actions in the European and Mediterranean theaters showcased the versatility and effectiveness of this exceptional commando force.

In 1944, recognizing the changing nature of the war and the need for specialized units, the Devil's Brigade was disbanded. However, its legacy lived on in the formation of modern special forces units, with the experiences and lessons learned by the 1st Special Service Force influencing the development of future elite military groups.

The Devil's Brigade remains a symbol of innovation and adaptability, representing a remarkable collaboration between the United States and Canada during a critical period in World War II. Their distinctive training, exceptional skills, and successful missions contribute to their status as one of the most renowned and respected special forces units in history.

101st Airborne

The 101st Airborne Division, also known as the "Screaming Eagles," was a highly esteemed and iconic American military unit that played a crucial role in World War II. Renowned for its bravery, tenacity, and exceptional training, the 101st Airborne was instrumental in some of the most critical campaigns of the war.

Activated in August 1942, the 101st Airborne Division was formed with the specific purpose of becoming an elite airborne infantry unit. Under the leadership of Major General William C. Lee, the division underwent rigorous training in parachute jumps, glider operations, and combat tactics. Their distinctive shoulder sleeve insignia, depicting an eagle with its wings spread, earned them the nickname "Screaming Eagles."

The 101st Airborne Division's first major combat operation in World War II was during the Allied invasion of Normandy on June 6, 1944, famously known as D-Day. As part of the larger airborne assault, the 101st Airborne was tasked with capturing key objectives behind enemy lines. The paratroopers dropped into the darkness of night, facing intense enemy fire and chaotic conditions. Despite the challenges, they successfully secured critical bridges and roads, preventing German reinforcements from reaching the beaches and playing a vital role in the success of the Normandy invasion.

Following their success in Normandy, the 101st Airborne Division continued to demonstrate their exceptional skills in subsequent operations. One of their most famous engagements was during the Battle of the Bulge in December 1944. The division was strategically positioned in the Ardennes region when the Germans launched a surprise offensive. Under severe weather conditions and surrounded by the enemy, the "Screaming Eagles" fiercely defended the town of Bastogne, refusing to surrender despite being vastly outnumbered. Their resilience and determination earned them widespread admiration and solidified their place in history.

Throughout the war, the 101st Airborne Division participated in numerous campaigns, including the liberation of Holland during Operation Market Garden and the capture of Hitler's mountain retreat, the Eagle's Nest, in Berchtesgaden, Germany.

The division's contributions in World War II came at a high cost. The soldiers of the 101st Airborne endured significant casualties, and many brave men made the ultimate sacrifice for their country. However, their courage and selflessness in the face of danger earned them a place of honor in the annals of American military history.

After the war, the 101st Airborne Division continued its legacy as an elite airborne unit and played critical roles in subsequent conflicts, including the Vietnam War and the Gulf War. Today, the division remains an active and highly regarded unit in the United States Army, known for its rapid deployment capabilities and specialized training.

The 101st Airborne Division's contributions in World War II not only demonstrated the power and effectiveness of airborne operations but also symbolized the bravery and dedication of American soldiers during one of the most significant conflicts in human history. Their legacy as the "Screaming Eagles" continues to inspire and uphold the values of courage, honor, and service to the nation.

Easy Company

Easy Company, officially known as E Company, 2nd Battalion, 506th Parachute Infantry Regiment, 101st Airborne Division, played a significant role in World War II. This group of extraordinary men became legendary for their bravery, resilience, and camaraderie in the face of unimaginable challenges during the war. Their experiences were later immortalized in the book "Band of Brothers" by Stephen E. Ambrose, which was also adapted into a critically acclaimed television miniseries.

Formed in 1942, Easy Company underwent rigorous training in preparation for their role as paratroopers. They were part of the elite 101st Airborne Division, known as the "Screaming Eagles," and were trained for airborne assaults and dangerous missions behind enemy lines. Their training instilled a strong sense of brotherhood and trust, forming the foundation of their resilience in the battles ahead.

One of Easy Company's most crucial missions was during the D-Day invasion on June 6, 1944. As part of Operation Overlord, they were tasked with parachuting into Normandy in the early hours of the morning. Facing intense enemy fire and adverse weather conditions, the men of Easy Company landed scattered across the French countryside. Despite this, they regrouped and accomplished their objectives, securing strategic positions and clearing enemy defenses to support the Allied landings on Utah Beach.

After their success in Normandy, Easy Company was involved in the fierce Battle of Carentan. This battle, fought in the heart of Normandy, saw the paratroopers engage in intense urban combat against determined German defenders. The capture of Carentan was vital in linking the Utah and Omaha Beachheads and allowed for a more cohesive Allied front in the Normandy campaign.

Easy Company's next major engagement was during Operation Market Garden in the Netherlands. As part of the largest airborne operation in history, they parachuted into Holland to capture key bridges and secure a pathway to Germany. However, the operation faced stiff resistance from German forces, and Easy Company found themselves surrounded and cut off during the Battle of Arnhem. Despite the odds, they held their ground and fought bravely, earning admiration for their unwavering determination.

One of the most harrowing experiences for Easy Company came during the Battle of the Bulge in the winter of 1944. As the Germans launched a surprise offensive in the Ardennes region, the paratroopers endured bitterly cold weather and constant enemy attacks. Despite being heavily outnumbered and surrounded, they held the line and played a crucial role in halting the German advance.

As the war drew to a close, Easy Company liberated the Kaufering IV sub-camp of the Dachau concentration camp in April 1945. Witnessing the horrors of the Holocaust firsthand deeply affected the men, leaving an enduring mark on their lives.

Throughout their time in combat, Easy Company faced devastating losses and unimaginable challenges, but their courage and resilience remained steadfast. Their unwavering dedication to one another and to their mission earned them the admiration and respect of their fellow soldiers and the world.

Nurses of Pearl Harbor

On the morning of December 7, 1941, the tranquility of the Hawaiian paradise of Pearl Harbor was shattered by a devastating surprise attack launched by the Japanese. As the bombs rained down and chaos ensued, a group of courageous and dedicated nurses found themselves thrust into the heart of the disaster. The Nurses of Pearl Harbor became unsung heroes, showcasing their unwavering commitment and selflessness in the face of unimaginable tragedy, ultimately saving countless lives.

In the early hours of that infamous day, as the Japanese bombers struck the naval base, hospitals and medical facilities were among the primary targets. The nurses stationed at the various medical centers faced an unprecedented crisis as they raced to respond to the mass casualties and injured personnel flooding their wards.

Undeterred by the danger and destruction surrounding them, the Nurses of Pearl Harbor worked tirelessly, employing their medical expertise and nurturing touch to treat the wounded and comfort the dying. With limited resources and overwhelming casualties, they exhibited incredible resilience and adaptability, using makeshift medical stations to provide life-saving care.

Many nurses displayed acts of heroism and bravery as they put their own lives at risk to save others. Amidst the constant threat of additional attacks, they navigated through smoke-filled corridors and debris-strewn areas to reach patients and deliver critical aid. Their dedication to duty was unwavering, and their quick thinking and calm demeanor in the midst of chaos proved vital in preserving the lives of those under their care.

As the sun set on that tragic day, the Nurses of Pearl Harbor had treated countless wounded and dying servicemen, playing a pivotal role in stabilizing the situation and providing a sense of hope amid the devastation. Their actions extended far beyond their professional duties; they offered emotional support to traumatized soldiers, helping them cope with the aftermath of the brutal assault.

The contributions of the Nurses of Pearl Harbor often went unrecognized amidst the broader narrative of the attack. However, their bravery and resilience did not go unnoticed by those they served. Countless servicemen later expressed their gratitude for the selfless efforts of these courageous nurses, acknowledging the crucial role they played in saving lives and providing comfort during a time of unprecedented crisis.

The events of that fateful day would have a profound impact on the Nurses of Pearl Harbor. Many of them continued to serve throughout the war, tending to the wounded on distant battlefields, while others returned to their civilian lives with a newfound appreciation for the value of their profession and the strength of their calling.

In conclusion, the Nurses of Pearl Harbor emerged as unsung heroes on that fateful day, displaying unparalleled courage and selflessness in the face of unimaginable tragedy. Their unwavering commitment to saving lives and providing comfort amid chaos showcased the true essence of their profession. These remarkable women deserve to be remembered and honored for their indispensable role in easing the suffering of the wounded and offering hope during one of the darkest chapters in American history.

Merrill's Marauders

Merrill's Marauders, officially known as the 5307th Composite Unit (Provisional), was a unique and elite American infantry unit that played a pivotal role in the China-Burma-India Theater during World War II. Established in 1943, this special unit was named after its commander, Brigadier General Frank Merrill, and it undertook a daring and challenging mission behind enemy lines in the jungles of Burma.

Tasked with the formidable objective of disrupting Japanese communication and supply lines, Merrill's Marauders embarked on a grueling and hazardous journey through the unforgiving terrain of the Burmese jungles. Their mission was to support the larger Allied efforts in the region and halt the Japanese advance into India. Operating in extremely challenging conditions, the Marauders faced not only the relentless natural obstacles of the jungle but also the constant threat of enemy patrols and ambushes.

One of the distinctive features of Merrill's Marauders was their status as a long-range penetration unit. This meant that they operated deep within enemy territory, often far from friendly lines, and had to rely on airdrops for supplies. The Marauders were trained to endure extended periods without traditional logistical support, showcasing their exceptional resilience and adaptability in the face of adversity.

The unit consisted of approximately 3,000 men, primarily drawn from the 5307th Composite Unit. Comprising volunteers from various divisions, including the 6th and 5307th Infantry Regiments, the Marauders represented a diverse and determined group of soldiers. Their training emphasized guerrilla warfare tactics, survival skills, and the ability to navigate the challenging terrain of the Burmese jungles.

In 1944, Merrill's Marauders faced their greatest challenge during the Burma Campaign. The unit undertook a hazardous march, known as the "Marauder Stilwell," covering over 1,000 miles in five months. This extraordinary trek through dense jungles and over rugged mountains aimed to cut off Japanese supply routes and disrupt their offensive plans in the region.

The Marauders faced numerous hardships during their mission, including malnutrition, disease, and the constant threat of Japanese ambushes. Despite these challenges, their determination and tenacity never wavered. Their actions significantly contributed to the larger Allied strategy in the Pacific theater, preventing the Japanese from advancing further into India and providing a crucial boost to the overall war effort.

Merrill's Marauders demonstrated exceptional bravery and resilience in the face of adversity. Their unique and daring mission showcased the importance of specialized units in unconventional warfare. The legacy of Merrill's Marauders lives on as a testament to the courage and sacrifice of these exceptional soldiers who played a vital role in the Allied victory in the Pacific during World War II.

In conclusion, Merrill's Marauders were a remarkable and unconventional unit that operated deep behind enemy lines in the challenging terrain of the Burmese jungles. Their mission, marked by endurance, adaptability, and courage, significantly contributed to the Allied victory in the China-Burma-India Theater during World War II.

Gurkha Troops

Gurkha troops, renowned for their bravery, loyalty, and distinctive curved knives known as kukris, played a significant role in World War II as part of the British and Indian armies. These soldiers, hailing from the hills of Nepal, formed a formidable force known for their exceptional combat skills and unwavering dedication to their commanders.

During World War II, Gurkha troops served in various theaters of war, including North Africa, Italy, Southeast Asia, and Burma. Their reputation for fearlessness and tenacity made them invaluable assets to the Allied forces. Gurkhas were known not only for their combat prowess but also for their resilience in adverse conditions, whether navigating dense jungles, scaling treacherous mountains, or enduring extreme weather.

One of the distinguishing features of Gurkha troops was their loyalty to the British Crown, a tradition that dates back to the early 19th century. The bond between Gurkhas and the British Army was formalized through recruitment agreements, and it has endured for generations. This deep sense of loyalty and camaraderie contributed to the effectiveness of Gurkha units on the battlefield.

Gurkha soldiers were equipped with the kukri, a traditional Nepalese knife with a distinct inwardly curved blade. The kukri was not only a formidable weapon in hand-to-hand combat but also a symbol of the Gurkhas' identity and heritage. The reputation of the kukri-wielding Gurkha became legendary, striking fear into the hearts of their adversaries.

In the harsh terrain of Burma, Gurkha troops faced particularly challenging conditions. The dense jungles and rugged mountains of Burma tested the mettle of any soldier, but the Gurkhas' expertise in mountain warfare and jungle survival gave them a strategic advantage. Their ability to navigate difficult terrain and engage in guerrilla-style warfare made them well-suited for the challenges presented by the Burma Campaign.

The Gurkhas also played a crucial role in the defense of India during the war. With their homeland situated between British India and the Axis powers in Asia, Gurkha units were instrumental in safeguarding the strategically important region. They faced the Japanese forces in intense battles along the Burma-India border, showcasing their resilience and combat effectiveness.

One of the most well-known Gurkha actions during World War II was the Battle of Imphal in 1944. Gurkha units fought alongside British and Indian troops against the Japanese, successfully repelling the enemy and contributing to the turning point in the Burma Campaign. Their bravery in the face of adversity earned them widespread admiration and respect.

After the war, Gurkha units continued to serve in various conflicts and peacekeeping missions, solidifying their reputation as elite and dependable soldiers. The legacy of Gurkha troops in World War II remains a testament to their courage, skill, and unwavering dedication to duty.

In conclusion, Gurkha troops played a vital role in World War II, demonstrating exceptional bravery and skill in diverse theaters of war. Their loyalty to the British Crown, proficiency in challenging terrains, and iconic use of the kukri set them apart as a formidable force. The Gurkhas' contributions to the Allied victory in World War II and their enduring legacy as elite soldiers underscore the impact of these remarkable warriors on the course of history.

Navajo Code Talkers

During World War II, amidst the chaos of battlefields and the ever-advancing technology of warfare, a group of Native American soldiers played an instrumental role in securing victory for the United States. Known as the Navajo Code Talkers, these brave men from the Navajo Nation developed an ingenious and unbreakable code that confounded the enemy and revolutionized military communication.

The Navajo Code Talkers were recruited by the U.S. Marine Corps in 1942 to serve as radio operators and messengers in the Pacific Theater. The Marines selected Navajo volunteers for this crucial mission due to their Native language's complexity and the code's indecipherable nature to outsiders. The code was based on their unwritten language, one of the most intricate and unique spoken languages in the world. Its complex syntax and phonetic qualities made it nearly impossible for non-Navajo speakers to understand, providing a significant advantage in wartime communication.

To create the code, the Navajo Code Talkers devised a system that assigned specific English words to Navajo terms representing military jargon and equipment. For instance, the Navajo word for "turtle" stood for "tank," and "chicken hawk" represented "dive bomber." This approach not only ensured the code's effectiveness but also maintained its security, as the Navajo code was never written down, making it immune to codebreaking efforts.

Deployed across the Pacific Theater, from Guadalcanal to Iwo Jima, the Navajo Code Talkers skillfully transmitted critical messages, orders, and coordinates without fear of interception. Even during intense battles, they remained calm and focused, ensuring the safety and efficiency of their communication lines. The Navajo Code Talkers' contributions significantly contributed to the Allied Forces' success in crucial battles, saving countless lives and leading to pivotal victories.

Despite their vital role in the war effort, the Navajo Code Talkers' contributions remained classified and shrouded in secrecy for many years. It wasn't until 1968 that their efforts were publicly acknowledged, and they received the recognition they so rightfully deserved. President Ronald Reagan awarded the original 29 Code Talkers with the prestigious Congressional Gold Medal, and subsequent groups of Code Talkers have also received this honor.

Beyond their role in the war, the Navajo Code Talkers' impact extended far beyond military service. Their remarkable achievements helped change perceptions of Native Americans, fostering a sense of pride and respect for their culture and contributions. Moreover, their service bolstered the broader acceptance of Native American languages, dispelling stereotypes about their supposed inferiority.

In conclusion, the Navajo Code Talkers remain an integral part of World War II history and an inspiring testament to human ingenuity and resilience in the face of adversity. Their unwavering dedication to their country, innovative code, and exceptional bravery on the battlefield ensured Allied victory in the Pacific Theater. The legacy of the Navajo Code Talkers continues to be celebrated, serving as a reminder of the remarkable contributions that can arise from diverse cultures and backgrounds united in a common cause.

Nisei Soldiers

During World War II, while the United States faced immense challenges on the battlefield, it also grappled with issues of discrimination and prejudice on the home front. The Nisei soldiers, second-generation Japanese Americans, played a crucial role in reshaping perceptions and contributing significantly to the US war effort. Despite facing racism and doubts about their loyalty, the Nisei soldiers demonstrated unwavering patriotism and bravery, leaving an indelible mark on American history.

When the Japanese attacked Pearl Harbor in 1941, Japanese Americans suddenly found themselves under scrutiny and suspicion. The government's fear of potential espionage and sabotage led to the internment of over 120,000 Japanese Americans, including many Nisei, in relocation camps across the country. However, this did not deter the Nisei from proving their allegiance to the United States.

In 1943, the War Department established the 442nd Regimental Combat Team, composed primarily of Nisei volunteers. The 442nd, along with the 100th Infantry Battalion (composed of Nisei and Hawai'i-born Japanese Americans), became some of the most decorated units in US military history. Despite facing prejudice and being segregated from other units, the Nisei soldiers demonstrated exceptional bravery and determination in battle.

The Nisei soldiers' most notable achievement came during the rescue of the "Lost Battalion" in the Vosges Mountains of France in 1944. The 442nd endured intense combat for six days, overcoming challenging terrain and fierce resistance from German forces. Their heroic efforts saved over 200 soldiers from the encircled 36th Infantry Division, at the cost of heavy casualties. The courage and sacrifice displayed by the Nisei soldiers during this battle earned them respect and recognition from their fellow servicemen and the American public.

Despite facing adversity, the Nisei soldiers maintained their loyalty and dedication to the US war effort. Their valor in combat dispelled the notion that Japanese Americans were disloyal, and their contributions had a significant impact on changing perceptions of their community. The Nisei soldiers' success in the face of discrimination helped pave the way for future generations of Japanese Americans to earn acceptance and respect in American society.

The 442nd and 100th Infantry Battalion's accomplishments also had a strategic significance. Their bravery and tenacity earned them the nickname "Go for Broke" for their willingness to risk everything for victory. The Nisei soldiers' combat prowess was instrumental in breaking through heavily fortified German defenses, leading to important victories for the Allies in Italy, France, and Germany. Their combat skills and unwavering determination were essential in securing the US war effort in the European Theater.

Furthermore, the Nisei soldiers' efforts had a profound impact on the Japanese American community, inspiring pride and fostering a stronger sense of identity. Their accomplishments provided a symbol of hope and resilience for those interned and facing discrimination back home. Many Nisei soldiers returned from the war with a newfound determination to fight for civil rights and work towards equality.

The Ghost Army

The Ghost Army, a clandestine unit of the United States Army during World War II, stands as a remarkable and unconventional chapter in military history. Operating from 1944 to 1945, this unique force was tasked with an extraordinary mission: to deceive and mislead Axis forces through a combination of artistic and tactical ingenuity.

Comprising artists, designers, and sound engineers, the Ghost Army was assembled with the goal of utilizing creative deception to confuse the enemy about the size, location, and activities of Allied military units. At the heart of their operations was the deployment of inflatable decoys, including tanks, trucks, and artillery, designed to mimic the presence of a formidable military division. Crafted with meticulous attention to detail, these inflatable props, often indistinguishable from real equipment from a distance, played a crucial role in the Ghost Army's overall strategy.

Operating in conjunction with these visual deceptions, the unit employed audio tactics to further enhance the illusion. Scripted radio transmissions, simulated sounds of troop movements, and other auditory effects were orchestrated to create the convincing impression of a large and active military force. The integration of both visual and auditory elements contributed to the Ghost Army's success in diverting enemy attention away from actual Allied operations.

One of the pivotal moments in the Ghost Army's deployment was during the lead-up to the Normandy landings in 1944. The unit played a critical role in the broader Allied strategy by deceiving German forces about the location and scale of the impending invasion. Inflatable tanks and other deceptive measures were strategically positioned to give the impression of a sizable Allied force massing at locations far removed from the actual D-Day landing sites.

The Ghost Army's activities extended beyond mere illusion, often involving daring maneuvers to draw enemy attention away from genuine troop movements. Members of the unit risked their lives by creating distractions and engaging in simulated actions, further emphasizing the commitment and resourcefulness of these unconventional soldiers.

Due to the classified nature of their operations, the Ghost Army's contributions remained largely unknown for decades after the war. It wasn't until the 1990s that their story was declassified and brought to public attention. The creativity, innovation, and audacity displayed by the Ghost Army underscored the importance of unconventional thinking in the theater of war.

The legacy of the Ghost Army endures as a testament to the power of ingenuity and artistic deception in military strategy. The unit's ability to use unconventional methods to achieve strategic goals highlights the adaptability and resourcefulness of those who served in this clandestine force. The Ghost Army's role in shaping the course of history during World War II remains a captivating and little-known chapter in the annals of military tactics and innovation, showcasing the impact of imagination and creativity on the battlefield.

French Resistance

In the tumultuous years of World War II, France found itself occupied by Nazi Germany, facing unimaginable challenges under the oppressive rule. However, amidst the darkness of the occupation, a beacon of hope emerged in the form of the French Resistance. This clandestine movement, comprising brave men and women, played a crucial role in resisting the Nazi regime, preserving their national identity, and supporting the Allied forces.

The French Resistance was a network of individuals and groups who defied the German occupation and its collaborators. These brave souls were known as "resistants" and operated covertly, engaging in acts of sabotage, intelligence gathering, and propaganda distribution. The Resistance members came from all walks of life - students, farmers, intellectuals, and even clergy - united by their unwavering determination to liberate their beloved country.

The Resistance carried out various acts of defiance against the German forces. Sabotaging railways, communication lines, and factories were common tactics employed by these courageous individuals. By disrupting the Nazis' logistical operations, the Resistance hindered their ability to wage war and weakened their grip on the occupied territories.

One of the pivotal roles of the French Resistance was gathering and transmitting intelligence to the Allies. They risked their lives to collect critical information on German troop movements, military installations, and strategic plans. This intelligence was of immense value to the Allies, providing them with vital insights into the enemy's strategies and aiding in their efforts to plan and execute military operations effectively.

In addition to their military efforts, the Resistance also played a significant role in fostering morale among the French population. They distributed underground newspapers and pamphlets, urging citizens to stand firm and resist the oppressive regime. These courageous acts of propaganda helped boost the people's spirits, reminding them that they were not alone in their fight for freedom.

The French Resistance operated under constant threat of discovery and faced severe repercussions if caught by the German authorities. Despite this, they demonstrated incredible resilience and bravery. They developed intricate networks of safe houses and secret meeting places to evade detection and capture. Their dedication to the cause and willingness to make personal sacrifices for the greater good earned them the respect and admiration of their fellow countrymen.

The Resistance's contributions to the Allied war effort cannot be overstated. By keeping the German occupiers preoccupied and weakened, they played a crucial role in paving the way for the eventual liberation of France. As the Allied forces gained momentum in their push toward victory, the Resistance rose in prominence and became a symbol of hope and determination for the French people.

In conclusion, the French Resistance was a heroic movement during World War II that demonstrated unwavering courage and defiance in the face of tyranny. Through acts of sabotage, intelligence gathering, and propaganda distribution, they played a crucial role in weakening the German occupation and supporting the Allied forces. Their sacrifices and dedication not only helped liberate France but also left an indelible mark on the nation's history, serving as a testament to the power of unity and resilience in the face of adversity.

Hitler Youth Program

The Hitler Youth Program, established by Adolf Hitler in 1922 and later officially named the Hitlerjugend in 1926, was a Nazi initiative designed to indoctrinate German youth into the ideology of the Nazi Party. The program played a significant role in shaping the beliefs and values of the younger generation in Nazi Germany.

The Hitler Youth aimed to mold young minds early, promoting loyalty to Hitler, racial purity, militarism, and unquestioning obedience to authority. It targeted boys aged 14 to 18, with the goal of preparing them for roles as future leaders, soldiers, and supporters of the Nazi regime.

Membership in the Hitler Youth became mandatory in 1936, and participation was highly encouraged for girls as well through the parallel organization known as the League of German Girls (BDM). The program was structured to provide a sense of belonging, purpose, and identity to its members, instilling Nazi ideals through a variety of activities.

One of the primary focuses of the Hitler Youth was militarization. Boys participated in military drills, physical training, and weapons education to prepare them for their future roles in the armed forces. The program aimed to create a generation of disciplined and obedient soldiers who would serve the Nazi state without question.

Beyond military training, the Hitler Youth engaged in various activities promoting Nazi ideology. These included ideological classes, where members were taught about the superiority of the Aryan race, anti-Semitism, and the principles of National Socialism. Indoctrination was reinforced through propaganda, emphasizing the importance of sacrificing personal desires for the collective goals of the Nazi state.

Sports and physical fitness were integral components of the Hitler Youth experience. The emphasis on athleticism served a dual purpose: it not only aimed to cultivate physically fit individuals but also reinforced the idea of competition, hierarchy, and the survival of the fittest—a reflection of Nazi racial theories.

Participation in the Hitler Youth was not limited to theoretical and physical training; it extended to community service and social activities. Members were encouraged to engage in volunteer work, participate in marches and parades, and attend events that celebrated Nazi ideals. The communal nature of these activities fostered a sense of camaraderie and belonging among the youth.

As World War II progressed, the Hitler Youth became increasingly involved in supporting the war effort. Older members were drafted into military service, while younger members were engaged in activities such as collecting scrap metal, distributing propaganda, and assisting in air raid precautions. The Hitler Youth's role in the war effort highlighted its function as a tool for mobilizing and utilizing the younger population in service to the Nazi regime.

The Hitler Youth program faced a decline towards the end of World War II, as Germany faced defeat and the Allied forces advanced. As the Nazi regime crumbled, the Hitler Youth played a minor role in the defense of Berlin, with young members often involved in futile attempts against the overwhelming Allied forces.

The legacy of the Hitler Youth remains a dark chapter in history, illustrating the extent to which authoritarian regimes can manipulate and exploit the youth for ideological purposes. The program's impact on the German youth, both in terms of indoctrination and the sacrifices made during the war, is a somber reminder of the dangers of using education and youth organizations as tools for propagating extremist ideologies.

German Panzer Divisions

The German Panzer Divisions, renowned for their formidable armored forces, played a crucial role in the military strategy of Nazi Germany during World War II. These divisions were instrumental in the Blitzkrieg tactics that characterized the early stages of the war, marking a significant shift in armored warfare.

A Panzer Division was a combined arms unit that included tanks (Panzer), infantry, and artillery, providing the German military with a highly mobile and powerful force. The concept of Panzer Divisions emerged in the interwar period as German military theorists, such as Heinz Guderian, emphasized the importance of mechanized and fast-moving armored units.

The German Panzer Divisions were central to the Blitzkrieg, a military strategy characterized by the rapid and coordinated movement of mechanized forces, including tanks, infantry, and air support. This strategy aimed to create a breakthrough in enemy lines, encircle opposing forces, and swiftly advance, leaving the enemy disoriented and unable to mount an effective defense.

Each Panzer Division typically consisted of several Panzer regiments, motorized infantry, self-propelled artillery, and support units. The Panzer regiments comprised various types of tanks, with the iconic Panzer IV and Panzer III serving as the backbone of these divisions. These tanks were well-armored and equipped with powerful guns, providing the German military with a formidable armored force.

The German Panzer Divisions saw significant action in the early campaigns of World War II, including the invasions of Poland, France, and the Low Countries. Their success was attributed to a combination of well-coordinated tactics, superior tank design, and highly trained crews. The speed and shock effect of the Blitzkrieg caught the opposing forces off guard, leading to swift victories for the German military.

One of the key strengths of the Panzer Divisions was their ability to adapt and evolve. As the war progressed, new tank models, such as the Tiger and Panther tanks, were introduced, enhancing the firepower and armor of the divisions. These heavy tanks were particularly effective against enemy armor and fortified positions.

The Eastern Front saw intense tank battles between the German Panzer Divisions and the Soviet armored forces. The wide-open spaces of the Eastern Front allowed for large-scale tank engagements, and the Panzer Divisions initially achieved considerable success. However, the harsh winter conditions and the sheer scale of the Eastern Front presented challenges for the German military.

Despite the initial successes, the German Panzer Divisions faced increasing difficulties as the war progressed. The Allied forces, particularly the Soviet Union and the Western Allies, developed effective countermeasures against Blitzkrieg tactics. Additionally, the German military industry struggled to match the production capabilities of the Allies, leading to a decline in the number of operational tanks.

By the later stages of the war, the German Panzer Divisions found themselves on the defensive, facing overwhelming odds on multiple fronts. The Battle of Kursk in 1943 marked a significant turning point on the Eastern Front, where the German offensive capabilities were blunted by the Soviet Red Army.

In conclusion, the German Panzer Divisions were instrumental in the early successes of Nazi Germany during World War II. Their innovative use of Blitzkrieg tactics and superior armored forces allowed for swift victories in the early campaigns. However, as the war progressed and the Allies adapted, the challenges facing the Panzer Divisions increased, ultimately contributing to the decline of Nazi Germany's military fortunes. The legacy of the Panzer Divisions remains a testament to the evolution of armored warfare and the impact of innovative military strategies.

The German Gestapo

The German Gestapo was a powerful organization during World War II. Led by Heinrich Himmler, it played a crucial role in maintaining the Nazi regime's control over Germany and occupied territories. The term "Gestapo" stands for Geheime Staatspolizei, which translates to Secret State Police. This feared agency was responsible for suppressing opposition, enforcing Nazi policies, and ensuring the regime's security.

The Gestapo's primary mission was to identify and eliminate perceived threats to the Nazi government. They utilized an extensive network of informants to gather information about individuals who were suspected of being enemies of the state. These informants could be neighbors, colleagues, or even family members, creating an atmosphere of suspicion and fear within society.

Once identified, individuals targeted by the Gestapo could face various forms of persecution. These ranged from arrests and interrogations to imprisonment and even execution. The Gestapo had the authority to detain people without trial, allowing them to imprison anyone they deemed a danger to the Nazi regime. Interrogations often involved harsh methods, and individuals were often subjected to physical and psychological torture to extract information or confessions.

The Gestapo's power extended beyond Germany's borders. In the occupied territories, they collaborated with local authorities to suppress resistance movements and dissent. Their brutal tactics, such as mass arrests and public executions, were meant to deter any form of opposition to the Nazi occupation.

The Gestapo was known for its meticulous record-keeping. They maintained extensive files on individuals and groups deemed to be enemies of the state. These records included personal information, political affiliations, and any perceived threats posed by the individuals. The information gathered was used to maintain control and to target specific individuals or groups for further action.

Fear was a powerful tool employed by the Gestapo. The constant threat of arrest, torture, or even death created an environment of silence and compliance. Many individuals chose to remain passive rather than risk drawing the attention of this feared organization. This atmosphere of fear and repression allowed the Nazi regime to consolidate its power and suppress any opposition effectively.

As World War II progressed, the Gestapo's role expanded to include the persecution of various groups, most notably Jews. They played a significant role in implementing the Holocaust, the systematic genocide of six million Jews. The Gestapo's involvement in this horrific crime highlights the depth of their commitment to the Nazi ideology and their willingness to carry out heinous acts.

In conclusion, the German Gestapo was a ruthless and powerful organization during World War II. With its reach extending across Germany and occupied territories, it maintained the Nazi regime's grip on power through fear, intimidation, and brutal suppression of opposition. The Gestapo's methods were characterized by arrests, interrogations, torture, and executions, leaving a dark and harrowing legacy in history.

The SS (Schutzstaffel)

The SS, or Schutzstaffel, was a paramilitary organization that played a significant and ominous role in Nazi Germany during World War II. Founded in 1925 as Adolf Hitler's personal bodyguard, the SS evolved into a powerful and multifaceted organization, becoming one of the principal instruments of terror and repression within the Nazi regime.

The origins of the SS can be traced back to the early days of the Nazi Party. Initially formed as a small unit responsible for Hitler's personal security, the SS expanded its scope and influence under the leadership of Heinrich Himmler. Himmler, who became the chief architect of the SS, transformed it into an organization that extended far beyond its original role.

The SS operated with a dual structure, comprising the Allgemeine SS and the Waffen-SS. The Allgemeine SS was responsible for internal security, ideological indoctrination, and enforcing racial purity policies. On the other hand, the Waffen-SS was the combat arm of the organization, consisting of military formations that fought alongside the regular German armed forces.

One of the SS's defining characteristics was its commitment to racial purity and the implementation of the Nazi racial ideology. The SS actively promoted the concept of Aryan superiority and sought to eliminate perceived "racial impurities." This led to policies such as forced sterilization, euthanasia programs, and ultimately, the genocide of millions during the Holocaust.

The SS played a central role in orchestrating the Final Solution, the systematic genocide of six million Jews and millions of others deemed undesirable by the Nazi regime. Himmler, as the head of the SS, oversaw the implementation of this horrific plan, coordinating the mass murder of innocent people in concentration and extermination camps. The efficiency with which the SS organized the logistics of mass extermination remains a dark chapter in human history.

The Waffen-SS, the combat arm of the organization, became notorious for its involvement in military campaigns and atrocities. Despite initially being formed as a military force separate from the regular German army, the Waffen-SS played a significant role in various theaters of war. Its units were involved in numerous war crimes, including the massacre of civilians and prisoners of war.

The SS also controlled the Gestapo, the secret police responsible for suppressing dissent and eliminating perceived threats to the Nazi regime. The Gestapo operated outside the legal constraints, using intimidation, torture, and extrajudicial executions to instill fear and maintain control. The SS's role in repression extended to concentration camps, where prisoners faced inhumane conditions, forced labor, and systematic extermination.

In the later stages of World War II, as Germany faced defeat, Himmler attempted to negotiate with the Allies to secure a separate peace. However, his efforts were in vain, and the SS found itself on the losing side of the conflict. In the aftermath of the war, the SS was declared a criminal organization by the Allied powers, and its leaders were prosecuted for war crimes and crimes against humanity during the Nuremberg Trials.

The legacy of the SS is one of infamy, symbolizing the darkest aspects of Nazi ideology and its implementation. The organization's involvement in genocide, repression, and militarized terror remains a stark reminder of the atrocities committed during the Holocaust and World War II. The SS's actions, under Himmler's leadership, stand as a testament to the consequences of unchecked extremism and the dangers of ideologies that prioritize racial purity over human dignity.

Waffen-SS

The Waffen-SS, the combat arm of the SS (Schutzstaffel), emerged as a formidable military force within Nazi Germany during World War II. Founded in 1933, the Waffen-SS played a significant role in various theaters of war and became notorious for its involvement in military campaigns, atrocities, and war crimes.

Initially conceived as a paramilitary force separate from the regular German army, the Waffen-SS evolved into a highly trained and well-equipped fighting force. Heinrich Himmler, the chief architect of the SS, envisioned the Waffen-SS as an elite unit that would embody the ideals of Aryan superiority and unwavering loyalty to Adolf Hitler.

One of the distinguishing features of the Waffen-SS was its dual role as both a combat force and a political entity. While maintaining military formations, the Waffen-SS also had a strong ideological component, emphasizing the commitment to Nazi racial doctrines and the ruthless pursuit of the goals set by the Nazi regime.

The Waffen-SS actively participated in early military campaigns, including the invasions of Poland and France. Its units displayed a combination of well-coordinated tactics, superior training, and the shock effect of Blitzkrieg, contributing to the swift victories achieved by Nazi Germany in the early stages of the war.

As the war progressed, the Waffen-SS became involved in numerous war crimes and atrocities. In the Eastern Front, particularly during the invasion of the Soviet Union, Waffen-SS units were responsible for mass killings of civilians, including Jews and other targeted groups. The brutal tactics employed by the Waffen-SS reflected the extreme ideology and militarized aggression of the Nazi regime.

One of the infamous units within the Waffen-SS was the Totenkopf (Death's Head) divisions, initially formed to guard concentration camps. These units later transitioned into combat roles and gained a reputation for their ruthlessness and brutality on the battlefield. The Totenkopf divisions were implicated in numerous atrocities, further tarnishing the image of the Waffen-SS.

Despite the involvement in war crimes, the Waffen-SS maintained a certain level of military prowess. Its soldiers received rigorous training, and the division incorporated various types of military equipment, including tanks and artillery. The Waffen-SS also attracted volunteers from various European countries, forming divisions with non-German personnel.

The reputation of the Waffen-SS, however, was marred by its association with atrocities, including the massacre of civilians, prisoners of war, and the implementation of the Final Solution. Its involvement in the Holocaust and brutal suppression of resistance movements in occupied territories contributed to the Waffen-SS being viewed as a symbol of Nazi militarized aggression.

In the later stages of World War II, as Germany faced setbacks on multiple fronts, the Waffen-SS experienced a decline in its operational capabilities. The Allied forces, including the Soviet Union and the Western Allies, developed effective countermeasures against Blitzkrieg tactics, and the Waffen-SS found itself on the defensive.

The legacy of the Waffen-SS remains one of infamy. Its involvement in war crimes and atrocities stains its military history, overshadowing any perceived military prowess. The Waffen-SS symbolizes the dark convergence of Nazi ideology and militarized aggression, emphasizing the dangers of ideological fervor within military institutions.

In conclusion, the Waffen-SS, as the combat arm of the SS, played a significant and notorious role in World War II. Initially conceived as an elite force embodying Nazi ideals, it became implicated in war crimes and atrocities. The Waffen-SS's military prowess was overshadowed by its association with brutal actions, and its legacy stands as a cautionary tale about the consequences of aligning military forces with extremist ideologies.

Spies & Secret Agents of WW II

World War II was not only fought on battlefields with armies and weapons; it was also a war of secrets and intelligence. Spies and secret agents played critical roles in gathering information, conducting covert operations, and making strategic decisions that had far-reaching impacts on the outcome of the war. These individuals operated behind enemy lines, often risking their lives to provide invaluable information and engage in espionage activities. The roles of spies and secret agents in World War II were diverse, and their significance cannot be underestimated.

One of the most famous spies of World War II was Richard "Dick" Chapman, also known as "The White Rabbit." Chapman was a British agent who worked as a double agent against the Germans. His role was to deceive German intelligence while secretly providing vital information to the British. His contributions helped mislead the Germans about the locations of Allied invasions, ultimately contributing to the success of D-Day.

Another renowned spy was Virginia Hall, an American woman who served as an undercover agent for both the British Special Operations Executive (SOE) and the American Office of Strategic Services (OSS). Known by the Gestapo as "The Limping Lady" due to her prosthetic leg, Hall operated in Nazi-occupied France. She organized resistance networks, provided critical intelligence, and coordinated sabotage operations that disrupted German supply lines and communication networks.

The significance of spies and secret agents in World War II was multifaceted. Firstly, their intelligence gathering provided Allied forces with critical information about enemy movements, plans, and capabilities. This information often proved vital in making strategic decisions and planning military operations. Spies helped detect and counter espionage activities of the Axis powers, preventing potentially catastrophic security breaches.

Secondly, secret agents played a pivotal role in espionage and sabotage operations behind enemy lines. These operations disrupted enemy communication, transportation, and supply chains, undermining their military effectiveness. Sabotage activities ranged from destroying key infrastructure to spreading misinformation, creating confusion among enemy ranks.

Moreover, the work of spies and secret agents extended beyond the battlefield. They gathered intelligence about enemy scientific research, technological advancements, and diplomatic negotiations. This information aided in shaping wartime policies, technological development, and post-war planning.

The contributions of spies and secret agents underscored the importance of intelligence gathering in modern warfare. The information they provided had a direct impact on military strategies, helping shape the course of battles and campaigns. Additionally, their efforts served as a testament to the lengths individuals were willing to go to defend their countries and uphold the values of freedom and democracy.

The roles and significance of spies and secret agents in World War II were substantial and diverse. Their intelligence gathering, covert operations, and bravery influenced military strategies, disrupted enemy plans, and played a crucial role in the outcome of the war. The stories of spies like Richard Chapman, Virginia Hall, and Oleg Gordievsky highlight the dedication, resourcefulness, and sacrifice of individuals who worked behind the scenes to ensure victory and safeguard the values of their nations.

Attack on Pearl Harbor

The Attack on Pearl Harbor, which occurred on the morning of December 7, 1941, stands as a pivotal event in world history and was a critical turning point that propelled the United States into World War II. This devastating surprise attack launched by the Japanese Imperial Navy on the American naval base in Hawaii had far-reaching consequences that reshaped the course of the war and the global geopolitical landscape.

At approximately 7:55 AM, the first wave of Japanese fighter planes and bombers commenced their assault on the United States Pacific Fleet stationed at Pearl Harbor. The attack targeted ships, aircraft, and military installations across the base. In a matter of minutes, the tranquil morning was shattered by the thunderous roar of explosions, the piercing cries of air raid sirens, and the plumes of smoke rising from the wreckage.

The attack resulted in the destruction of eight American battleships, including the USS Arizona and the USS Oklahoma, both of which were irreparably sunk. Numerous other ships and aircraft were heavily damaged or destroyed. In total, more than 2,400 Americans lost their lives, and around 1,200 were injured. The devastation was extensive, and the shock and grief that reverberated across the nation were profound.

The question of why Japan launched this brazen attack on the United States has been a subject of analysis and debate for decades. At the heart of Japan's motives were geopolitical and strategic ambitions. Japan sought to secure access to resources in Southeast Asia and the Pacific, and it believed that crippling the United States' Pacific Fleet would create a window of opportunity to achieve its objectives without facing significant American resistance.

The absence of American aircraft carriers at Pearl Harbor on the day of the attack was a pivotal factor that would later prove to be a significant advantage for the United States. The carriers, being the heart of the U.S. naval response, were not in port during the attack. This absence meant that while the battleships and installations suffered grave losses, the carriers remained unscathed. This proved crucial, as the carriers became the backbone of the U.S. Pacific Fleet's subsequent counteroffensive against Japan.

The significance of the Attack on Pearl Harbor was profound on multiple levels. Firstly, it shattered America's sense of security and isolationism, forcing the nation to acknowledge its vulnerability to external threats. The shock and outrage that followed led to an outpouring of national unity and resolve, as Americans rallied together to confront the challenge posed by the Axis powers.

Moreover, the attack directly prompted the United States to officially enter World War II. On December 8, 1941, the day after the attack, President Franklin D. Roosevelt addressed Congress, delivering his famous "Day of Infamy" speech, requesting a declaration of war against Japan. Congress swiftly granted the request, marking the United States' formal entrance into the global conflict.

The Attack on Pearl Harbor was a momentous event that reshaped the trajectory of World War II and the world at large. The audacious assault on the American naval base propelled the United States into the war, triggering a wave of national determination and resolve.

Doolittle Raid

Amidst the chaos of World War II, the Doolittle Raid emerged as a daring and significant military operation that bolstered American morale and dealt a strategic blow to Japan. Led by Lieutenant Colonel James "Jimmy" Doolittle, this audacious raid demonstrated the United States' determination to strike back after the devastating attack on Pearl Harbor and marked a pivotal turning point in the Pacific Theater of the war.

On December 7, 1941, the Japanese launched a surprise attack on the U.S. naval base at Pearl Harbor, Hawaii, resulting in the destruction of numerous American ships and aircraft and the loss of thousands of lives. The attack shook the nation and propelled the United States into World War II. The Doolittle Raid, planned in retaliation, aimed to strike back at Japan's heartland and demonstrate that the American military would not be defeated or deterred.

The Doolittle Raid involved a daring plan to launch a bombing raid on Tokyo and other Japanese cities from an aircraft carrier. This was an unprecedented and risky undertaking, as land-based bombers had never before taken off from an aircraft carrier due to the limited deck space. However, the brave and skilled pilots of the U.S. Army Air Forces were up to the challenge.

On April 18, 1942, sixteen B-25 Mitchell bombers, led by Lieutenant Colonel Doolittle, took off from the aircraft carrier USS Hornet and headed toward Japan. The aircraft faced numerous challenges, including limited fuel, which meant that they would not be able to return to the carrier after the bombing run. Instead, they planned to continue to friendly airfields in China or the Soviet Union.

The surprise attack on Tokyo was successful, and the Doolittle Raid inflicted significant damage on Japanese industrial and military targets. While the physical damage was not extensive, the psychological impact was profound. The Japanese military and civilians were stunned and humiliated that their homeland had been struck by an enemy considered so far away.

The Doolittle Raid had several significant effects on the course of the war. Firstly, it boosted American morale and provided a much-needed psychological lift after the devastating blow of Pearl Harbor. The raid demonstrated that the United States could take the fight to Japan and showed that the Japanese home islands were not invulnerable.

Secondly, the raid forced Japan to divert valuable military resources to defend its home islands. The fear of further attacks prompted the Japanese to keep some of their powerful naval fleet near their homeland instead of deploying it to confront the U.S. Navy in other areas of the Pacific. This diversion weakened Japan's offensive capabilities and provided the Allies with an advantage in subsequent battles.

Finally, the Doolittle Raid played a role in Japan's decision to plan and execute the Battle of Midway. The Japanese believed that by luring the U.S. Pacific Fleet into a decisive battle, they could secure their eastern defensive perimeter and force the United States to negotiate peace. However, the Battle of Midway proved disastrous for Japan, as the U.S. Navy dealt a severe blow to the Imperial Japanese Navy, turning the tide of the war in the Pacific in favor of the Allies.

Bataan Death March

The Bataan Death March was a harrowing and tragic event that occurred during World War II in the Philippines. It took place after the surrender of American and Filipino forces to the Japanese in April 1942, following months of intense fighting in the Battle of Bataan.

The Bataan Death March began on April 9, 1942, when approximately 75,000 American and Filipino prisoners of war were forced to march over 60 miles from the Bataan Peninsula to a Japanese internment camp near Capas, Tarlac. The march lasted for six days under brutal conditions, with prisoners subjected to extreme heat, little food or water, and relentless physical abuse from their captors.

The Japanese military had little regard for the well-being of the prisoners, viewing them as expendable and treating them with cruelty. Many prisoners were already weakened and suffering from malnutrition and illness due to the grueling battle and the harsh conditions of their captivity before the march even began.

During the march, prisoners endured atrocities and were subjected to various forms of abuse. Any prisoner who could not keep up with the pace was often beaten or killed on the spot. Those who fell behind were often bayoneted, shot, or beheaded. The Japanese soldiers showed little mercy, and the prisoners were forced to endure unimaginable suffering.

The prisoners faced not only physical torment but also emotional and psychological trauma. Many witnessed the deaths of comrades and were powerless to help them. The horror and suffering of the Bataan Death March left lasting scars on the survivors, haunting them for the rest of their lives.

Estimates vary, but it is believed that thousands of prisoners perished during the march due to execution, starvation, dehydration, and disease. The exact death toll remains uncertain, as many records were destroyed or hidden by the Japanese authorities after the war.

The Bataan Death March is considered one of the darkest chapters of World War II and a symbol of the cruelty and inhumanity of war. It became a rallying cry for those who survived and later fought to liberate the Philippines and defeat the Japanese forces in the Pacific.

After the war, the survivors of the Bataan Death March were honored for their courage and resilience. Memorials and monuments were erected in their memory, serving as reminders of the sacrifices made by those who endured this horrific ordeal.

The Bataan Death March stands as a solemn reminder of the atrocities of war and the importance of remembering the sacrifices of those who fought and suffered during World War II. It serves as a poignant lesson about the value of peace, compassion, and respect for human dignity in times of conflict. The memory of the Bataan Death March continues to evoke deep emotions and stands as a testament to the indomitable spirit of those who endured unimaginable hardships for the sake of their comrades and their countries.

Battle of Britain

In the summer of 1940, the Battle of Britain emerged as a pivotal and courageous chapter in World War II. This historic air campaign saw the Royal Air Force (RAF) of the United Kingdom facing off against the formidable Luftwaffe of Nazi Germany. The battle took place in the skies over Britain, as the Luftwaffe sought to gain air superiority and prepare the way for a planned invasion. The events of the Battle of Britain would become a symbol of British resilience and determination against overwhelming odds.

As World War II raged on, Nazi Germany began an ambitious military campaign to conquer Europe. Having defeated several nations and consolidated power on the continent, Hitler's next objective was to subdue the United Kingdom. Operation Sea Lion, the planned invasion of Britain, hinged upon the Luftwaffe neutralizing the RAF and establishing air supremacy.

The battle commenced on July 10, 1940, with the Luftwaffe launching relentless airstrikes on British coastal cities and airfields. The RAF, led by Air Chief Marshal Sir Hugh Dowding, responded with bravery and strategic prowess. The aircraft at the heart of the RAF's defense were the iconic Spitfire and Hurricane fighters, which proved to be agile and effective in the aerial dogfights.

Despite the Luftwaffe's numerical advantage, the RAF's resilience and innovative tactics played a crucial role in turning the tide of the battle. The British pilots demonstrated exceptional courage as they took to the skies day after day, engaging in intense aerial battles against the enemy. They employed the "Big Wing" strategy, grouping multiple squadrons to meet the German forces head-on, which proved effective in countering the Luftwaffe's attacks.

As the battle intensified, London and other British cities experienced relentless bombing in what became known as the Blitz. The Luftwaffe's goal was to break the British spirit through mass destruction, but the resilience of the British people only grew stronger. The RAF pilots and ground crews worked tirelessly to repair damaged aircraft and keep them operational, demonstrating their unwavering dedication to defending their homeland.

The turning point of the Battle of Britain came in September 1940. The Luftwaffe shifted its focus from RAF airfields to London, hoping to force the RAF into a decisive confrontation. However, this change in strategy played to the advantage of the British, as it gave the RAF valuable time to recover and regroup.

On September 15, 1940, a pivotal day in the battle, the Luftwaffe launched a massive assault on London, intending to deliver a knockout blow. Yet, the RAF, with their tenacity and courage, thwarted the attack and inflicted significant losses on the enemy. This day became known as "Battle of Britain Day" and marked a significant setback for the Luftwaffe.

Realizing the mounting casualties and the failure to gain air superiority, Hitler postponed the invasion of Britain indefinitely in October 1940. The RAF's victory in the Battle of Britain not only preserved the UK as a base for the Allies but also boosted the morale of the British people and proved to be a turning point in the course of World War II.

Battle of the Denmark Strait

In the midst of World War II, on May 24, 1941, a legendary naval engagement known as the Battle of the Denmark Strait took place in the cold waters of the North Atlantic. This battle ultimately led to the sinking of the mighty German battleship, the Bismarck, a turning point in the naval conflict between the Axis and Allied forces.

The confrontation unfolded at dawn when the Bismarck, a symbol of German naval power, and its companion cruiser, the Prinz Eugen, encountered a British task force. The British fleet consisted of the HMS Hood, one of the Royal Navy's most iconic ships, and the HMS Prince of Wales, a recently commissioned battleship. As the sun began to rise, the two sides prepared for battle.

At 5:52 AM, the Hood and the Prince of Wales fired their initial salvo at the German vessels. A fierce exchange of gunfire erupted, with the Hood targeting the Bismarck and the Prince of Wales engaging the Prinz Eugen. The German ships responded with precision, hitting the Hood with a devastating salvo that ignited an explosion in the ship's magazine. Tragically, the Hood, known as "The Mighty Hood," succumbed to the massive explosion and sank within minutes, leaving only a handful of survivors.

Realizing the severity of the situation, the British commander, Admiral John Tovey, rallied his forces to continue the pursuit of the Bismarck. Over the next few days, British reconnaissance planes spotted the Bismarck, despite its attempts to evade detection. On May 26, a daring Swordfish torpedo bomber attack launched from the aircraft carrier HMS Ark Royal hit the Bismarck's rudder, crippling its ability to steer effectively.

With the Bismarck's maneuverability severely impaired, the British fleet closed in for the final showdown. On May 27, the British battleships relentlessly pounded the Bismarck, causing significant damage to its guns, engines, and superstructure.

As hope dwindled, the German crew made the difficult decision to scuttle the ship to prevent it from falling into enemy hands.

In the early hours of May 27, the Bismarck's crew evacuated the ship as it rapidly took on water. A combined effort of British torpedoes and the inevitable sinking of the ship led to the final demise of the once-mighty battleship. Out of a crew of over 2,200, only around 110 survivors were rescued from the icy waters by British ships, marking the end of the Bismarck's short but impactful naval career.

The Battle and Sinking of the Bismarck highlighted the critical role of air power in naval warfare, as well as the importance of strategic planning and collaboration between naval forces. The loss of the Bismarck dealt a significant blow to the morale of the German Navy and boosted the spirits of the Allied forces, demonstrating their determination to challenge the Axis powers on all fronts.

In conclusion, the Battle of the Denmark Strait and the subsequent sinking of the Bismarck were pivotal moments in World War II's naval theater. The clash between the British and German ships showcased the sheer power and complexity of naval warfare during that era, with the Bismarck's fate serving as a reminder that even the mightiest vessels can be brought down through a combination of skill, determination, and strategic planning.

Battle of Midway

The Battle of Midway was a significant event during World War II in June 1942. It was a major clash between the United States and Japan in the Pacific Ocean near an island called Midway. This battle revolved around powerful aircraft carriers and had a great impact on the outcome of the war.

Aircraft carriers were like floating bases for airplanes. In the Battle of Midway, both the United States and Japan had these enormous ships. The United States had three carriers: the USS Enterprise, the USS Hornet, and the USS Yorktown. Japan had four carriers: the Akagi, Kaga, Soryu, and Hiryu. These carriers were crucial because they could launch planes that could fly great distances to attack enemy ships and bases.

The Battle of Midway is often remembered for its significance in shaping the course of the war. Before this battle, Japan had been successful in capturing territories across the Pacific. However, at Midway, the United States gained a decisive victory. They managed to sink four of Japan's aircraft carriers – the very heart of Japan's naval power. This weakened Japan's ability to wage war and turned the momentum in favor of the United States.

One of the key moments of the battle involved American codebreakers who deciphered Japanese secret messages. This intelligence allowed the United States to anticipate Japan's plans and movements. For instance, they knew the Japanese were planning to attack the island of Midway. This advance knowledge enabled the American forces to prepare and launch a successful counterattack.

The Battle of Midway was not just a clash of military might; it showcased the bravery and determination of the people involved. Many heroes emerged from this battle, both on the American and Japanese sides. American pilots like Lieutenant Commander Wade McClusky and Lieutenant Richard Best played critical roles by skillfully attacking the Japanese carriers, leading to their destruction.

In the grand scheme of the war, the Battle of Midway marked a turning point. It demonstrated the importance of naval air power and carrier-based aircraft. The United States showed its resilience and ability to stand up to Japan's advance. The battle also highlighted the significance of intelligence and strategy in warfare. By breaking the Japanese code, the Americans gained a key advantage that directly contributed to their victory.

In conclusion, the Battle of Midway was a pivotal event during World War II. Fought between the United States and Japan, this battle centered around powerful aircraft carriers that launched planes for combat. The outcome of the battle had a profound impact on the war. The United States' victory at Midway weakened Japan's naval strength and turned the tide of the war in the Pacific. This battle underscored the importance of intelligence, strategy, and bravery in achieving success on the battlefield.

Battle of Stalingrad

The Battle of Stalingrad was a critical and harrowing confrontation that unfolded during World War II. Taking place from August 23, 1942, to February 2, 1943, in the city of Stalingrad, Soviet Union (now Volgograd, Russia), this battle is known for its extreme weather conditions, relentless combat, and profound significance in shaping the outcome of the war.

The weather conditions during the Battle of Stalingrad were incredibly harsh and unforgiving. The battle occurred in the midst of the Soviet winter, subjecting soldiers to freezing temperatures that often dropped well below freezing point. The cold weather brought additional challenges, such as frostbite and reduced mobility due to frozen ground.

The opponents in the Battle of Stalingrad were the German Army, led by Field Marshal Friedrich Paulus, and the Soviet Red Army, under the command of General Georgy Zhukov. The Germans aimed to capture Stalingrad as part of their larger campaign to conquer the Soviet Union. The Soviets, however, were determined to defend their city and halt the German advance.

Both sides deployed various types of military units in the battle. The Germans brought armored units, infantry divisions, and elite soldiers like the Waffen-SS. The Soviets, on the other hand, employed infantry divisions, tank brigades, and their own elite troops. The nature of the battle made every type of unit crucial, as urban combat required a diverse range of skills and tactics.

The outcome of the Battle of Stalingrad was a turning point in World War II. The Soviets managed to encircle the German forces, effectively trapping them within the city. The German Army faced dire circumstances due to dwindling supplies, harsh weather, and the determined Soviet resistance. On February 2, 1943, the German Sixth Army, led by Field Marshal Paulus, surrendered, marking a significant victory for the Soviet Union.

The significance of the Battle of Stalingrad cannot be overstated. It marked a major shift in the course of World War II, as it halted the German advance into the Soviet Union and began the process of pushing the German forces back. The battle's outcome boosted Soviet morale and weakened the German military's momentum. It also set the stage for subsequent Soviet offensives that would eventually lead to the defeat of Nazi Germany.

In summary, the Battle of Stalingrad was a defining moment in World War II. Fought in brutal weather conditions, it pitted the German Army against the Soviet Red Army in a determined struggle for control of the city. The battle's outcome, with the surrender of the German Sixth Army, marked a turning point in the war and carried immense significance for both the Soviets and the Germans. The legacy of the Battle of Stalingrad continues to remind the world of the sacrifices and resilience displayed by those who fought in one of history's most pivotal conflicts.

Battle of Guadalcanal

The Battle of Guadalcanal stands as a pivotal moment in the Pacific Theater of World War II. Fought between the Allied forces, primarily the United States, and the Imperial Japanese Navy, this six-month-long campaign marked a turning point in the struggle for control over the Solomon Islands.

In August 1942, the Allies launched Operation Watchtower with the goal of capturing Guadalcanal, an island in the Solomon chain. This strategic move aimed to prevent the Japanese from using the island's airfield to threaten supply routes between the United States and Australia. The initial amphibious assault saw the Allies secure a foothold on the island, but the battle was far from over.

What followed was a fierce and grueling conflict characterized by naval battles, air raids, and intense ground fighting. The Japanese, determined to reclaim the island, launched multiple counterattacks in a bid to drive the Allies back into the sea. The Battle of Savo Island, a night naval engagement, resulted in heavy losses for the Allied fleet, underscoring the ferocity of the fighting.

On land, the battle unfolded in the jungles and swamps of Guadalcanal. Both sides faced harsh conditions, with disease, harsh weather, and rugged terrain adding to the challenges. The Battle of Bloody Ridge and the Battle of Edson's Ridge showcased the tenacity of both sides as they clashed in brutal close-quarter combat.

The naval conflict reached a climax with the Battle of Guadalcanal, a series of night engagements that saw the Allies successfully repel Japanese attempts to reinforce their forces on the island. This marked a significant turning point, as the Japanese were unable to break the Allied hold on Guadalcanal.

By February 1943, the Japanese finally abandoned their efforts to recapture Guadalcanal. The campaign had taken a heavy toll on both sides, with losses in ships, aircraft, and personnel.

The Battle of Guadalcanal was a hard-fought victory for the Allies, showcasing their determination to gain a strategic foothold in the Pacific.

The Battle of Guadalcanal had far-reaching consequences. It shattered the myth of Japanese invincibility and marked the first significant land defeat for Japan in the war. The Allies' success on Guadalcanal set the stage for further offensives in the Pacific, eventually leading to the rolling back of Japanese advances.

The battle's legacy endures as a testament to the courage and sacrifices of those who fought on both sides. The jungle-covered battlegrounds and the waters around Guadalcanal remain hallowed ground, a reminder of the fierce struggle for control of this remote island and the impact it had on the course of World War II.

Battle of the Atlantic

The Battle of the Atlantic was a crucial naval conflict that raged during World War II. This intense struggle took place in the vast waters of the Atlantic Ocean, where Allied forces faced off against German submarines, known as U-boats, in a bid to secure vital supply lines and protect their nations from hunger and defeat. Lasting from 1939 to 1945, the battle was marked by cunning tactics, advanced technology, and unwavering determination on both sides.

As German U-boats prowled the Atlantic's depths, they aimed to disrupt the transportation of goods between North America and Europe. The Allies depended on these supply lines to fuel their war effort, making the U-boats' mission a dire threat. The Germans employed a strategy called "wolfpack" tactics, in which groups of U-boats hunted together to overwhelm merchant convoys and military vessels. This approach allowed the U-boats to strike quickly and vanish beneath the waves, making them a formidable adversary.

In response, the Allies devised countermeasures to protect their convoys and weaken the U-boats' grip. They introduced innovative technologies such as sonar, which used sound waves to detect submerged submarines. This breakthrough provided Allied ships with the ability to locate U-boats even when hidden underwater. Additionally, long-range aircraft equipped with radar patrolled the skies, extending the Allies' reach and enabling them to pinpoint U-boats on the surface.

The battle's turning point came with the development of improved convoy tactics. The Allies organized their merchant ships into tight-knit groups, surrounded by warships that provided protection. This formation allowed the warships to guard the vulnerable cargo vessels, making it difficult for U-boats to single out their targets. As a result, the Allies managed to reduce the devastating losses they had previously endured.

However, the Battle of the Atlantic remained an arduous struggle. The U-boats continued to adapt, employing new tactics and technology to evade detection. They constructed faster submarines and even experimented with more advanced torpedoes that were harder to detect and could inflict more damage. The Allies responded by ramping up their production of ships, aircraft, and advanced weaponry, further escalating the arms race beneath the waves.

As the conflict raged on, the Allies gained the upper hand. They improved their intelligence gathering, which enabled them to decipher German naval codes and predict U-boat movements. This breakthrough allowed Allied ships and aircraft to intercept U-boats more effectively, leading to a gradual decline in their effectiveness. The Allies also established air and naval bases along key routes, extending their reach and limiting the U-boats' operational areas.

The Battle of the Atlantic reached its climax in 1943, as the combined efforts of the Allies began to weaken the U-boat threat. The U-boat losses became unsustainable for the Germans, and their dwindling resources hampered their ability to sustain the battle. By 1945, the Allied forces had secured their dominance, and the U-boat threat was largely neutralized.

In conclusion, the Battle of the Atlantic was a pivotal struggle that shaped the outcome of World War II. Through ingenious tactics, technological innovation, and sheer determination, the Allied forces managed to overcome the U-boat threat and secure the vital supply lines that sustained their war effort. This battle serves as a testament to the power of human ingenuity and collaboration in the face of immense challenges.

D-Day

D-Day, a key event during World War II, took place on June 6, 1944. On this day, Allied forces launched a massive operation to liberate Europe from the control of Nazi Germany. This operation involved a tremendous amount of planning and coordination, and it marked a turning point in the war.

The Allies, which included soldiers from the United States, the United Kingdom, Canada, and other countries, were determined to free Europe from the grasp of the Nazis. They chose to land on the beaches of Normandy, located in France, because it was a strategic starting point for their mission. The beaches were named Utah, Omaha, Gold, Juno, and Sword.

Before the main attack, brave paratroopers were dropped behind enemy lines to secure important locations and weaken the German defenses. These paratroopers were like the tip of the spear, helping to pave the way for the larger assault.

As the sun began to rise on June 6th, ships and boats carrying soldiers set sail for the Normandy beaches. The soldiers faced a tough challenge – the Germans had set up strong defenses along the coastline. The largest and most intense battle happened on Omaha Beach, where the Allies faced heavy gunfire and obstacles from the Germans. However, their determination and bravery pushed them forward, and they managed to break through the enemy's defenses.

The success of D-Day wasn't just about the soldiers on the ground. Before the invasion, the Allies carried out a massive bombardment of the German defenses along the coast. Ships fired shells, and planes dropped bombs to weaken the enemy's ability to fight back. This bombardment played a crucial role in giving the soldiers a better chance of success.

The number of troops involved in D-Day was astounding. Around 156,000 soldiers from different countries participated in the operation. The Allies also used more than 5,000 ships and over 11,000 planes to support the invasion. This shows how determined they were to free Europe from Nazi control.

D-Day was a remarkable display of teamwork and unity. Soldiers from various nations worked together to achieve a common goal – to defeat the Nazis and bring back freedom. This sense of unity and shared purpose was a driving force behind the success of the operation.

The impact of D-Day was enormous. The Allies managed to establish a strong foothold in Normandy, which allowed them to start pushing the Germans back. This marked the beginning of the end for Nazi Germany's control over Europe. The battles that followed D-Day were difficult and challenging, but the Allies kept fighting, determined to bring freedom to the people of Europe.

The sacrifices made on D-Day and in the battles that followed will never be forgotten. Many soldiers lost their lives, but their bravery and determination live on as an inspiration. D-Day remains a symbol of courage, unity, and the power of people coming together to overcome great odds.

Attack on Pointe du Hoc

The Battle of Ramree Island, a lesser-known but significant episode of World War II, unfolded in early 1945 and involved British and Indian forces against Japanese troops. Located in the Bay of Bengal, Ramree Island was the setting for a harrowing and brutal battle, best known for an unusual natural phenomenon that added to the horrors of war. This description offers a detailed look into the battle, its context, and its consequences.

By early 1945, the tide of World War II was turning against Japan. Allied forces were advancing steadily through Southeast Asia, seeking to reclaim territories occupied by Japanese forces. Ramree Island, part of British Burma (present-day Myanmar), became a crucial strategic point in this effort.

The Japanese had established a presence on Ramree Island, creating defenses and fortifications. The island was strategically significant as it provided control over the coastal waters, which were key for Japanese naval operations in the region.

In January 1945, British and Indian forces launched a military operation to liberate Ramree Island from Japanese control. The operation was codenamed "Operation Matador." Led by Major General Robert "Roy" Urquhart, the assault involved the 71st Indian Infantry Brigade, with support from naval and air forces.

The assault on Ramree Island commenced on January 14, 1945, with British and Indian troops landing on the island's beaches. Fierce fighting broke out as they encountered Japanese defenses. The dense mangrove swamps and thick vegetation on the island added to the challenges of the campaign.

As the battle raged on, the Japanese forces suffered significant casualties. Desperate to escape the advancing

Allied troops, many Japanese soldiers retreated into the mangrove swamps, hoping to evade capture. However, these mangroves were infested with saltwater crocodiles.

What ensued was a horrific natural tragedy as crocodiles attacked the Japanese soldiers who had taken refuge in the swamps. While estimates vary, it is believed that a significant number of Japanese soldiers fell victim to these reptiles. The actual number of casualties remains a subject of debate among historians, but the event has gained notoriety for its brutality.

Despite the deadly encounter with the crocodiles, the battle on Ramree Island continued, and the Allied forces ultimately succeeded in liberating the island. Japanese troops were either killed, captured, or forced to retreat.

The Battle of Ramree Island is remembered as a fierce and costly confrontation during the final stages of World War II in Southeast Asia. It is also known for the tragic episode of crocodile attacks, which is a chilling and unusual aspect of wartime history.

Today, Ramree Island is part of Myanmar and has returned to being a relatively peaceful and serene place. It serves as a reminder of the tumultuous past and the sacrifices made during the war. The island's natural beauty stands in stark contrast to the horrors of the battle.

Battle of Iwo Jima

The Battle of Iwo Jima stands as a defining moment in World War II's Pacific Theater, marked by valor, sacrifice, and strategic importance. Fought between the United States and the Empire of Japan from February 19 to March 26, 1945, this grueling conflict for control of the Japanese island of Iwo Jima had far-reaching consequences.

Iwo Jima, a small volcanic island located midway between Japan and the Mariana Islands, held immense significance for both sides. The U.S. sought to secure it as a vital base for airfields that could provide strategic advantages in bombing mainland Japan. The Japanese recognized its defensive value and were determined to thwart American advances.

The initial assault by American forces faced fierce resistance. The Japanese had fortified the island with an intricate network of tunnels, bunkers, and defensive positions. This well-prepared defense created significant challenges for the U.S. Marines tasked with landing on the island's beaches.

The battle's iconic image—an American flag being raised atop Mount Suribachi—captured the spirit of determination and sacrifice that defined the struggle. However, the battle extended beyond this moment, with intense and brutal fighting continuing across the island's rugged terrain.

The battle on Iwo Jima unfolded in harsh conditions. The island's black volcanic sand, combined with the complex network of Japanese defenses, made the progress of American forces slow and arduous. The engagement tested the resolve of both sides, with the U.S. forces demonstrating unwavering determination to press forward despite heavy casualties.

After weeks of relentless fighting, the U.S. Marines finally managed to secure the island. However, victory came at a high cost—over 6,800 American lives were lost, and many more were wounded. The Japanese forces suffered near-total annihilation, with only a handful of prisoners captured.

The Battle of Iwo Jima had profound implications for the course of the war. The capture of the island allowed the U.S. to establish airfields that significantly shortened the distance to Japan, enabling more frequent and effective bombing raids. This, coupled with other military successes, contributed to the eventual defeat of Japan.

The legacy of the Battle of Iwo Jima endures in the collective memory of both nations. The iconic flag-raising photograph became a symbol of American valor and determination. The battle's significance extends beyond its military impact, serving as a reminder of the human cost of war and the sacrifices made by those who fought on both sides. The island itself remains a solemn memorial to the sacrifices of all those who participated in this historic conflict.

Battle of the Bulge

The Battle of the Bulge was a significant military clash that unfolded during World War II. This intense struggle occurred in the winter of 1944 in the Ardennes region of Europe. It involved Allied forces, led by the United States, Britain, and other nations, facing off against the German military in a last-ditch effort by the Germans to turn the tide of the war. The battle was marked by surprise attacks, harsh weather conditions, and a determined fight on both sides.

The Battle of the Bulge derived its name from the unique way the frontlines shifted during the battle. The Germans launched a surprise attack that created a bulge-like shape in the Allied lines, leading to the name "bulge." The Germans' goal was to divide the Allied forces, capture vital supply ports, and ultimately force the Allies to negotiate a separate peace.

The Germans chose the Ardennes region for their attack due to its dense forests and hilly terrain. This area was lightly defended by the Allies, who believed it was an unlikely location for a large-scale offensive. The element of surprise favored the Germans initially, as they caught the Allied forces off guard and managed to make significant gains.

Despite the initial success, the Germans faced challenges. Harsh winter weather, including heavy snowfall and freezing temperatures, slowed their progress. The same conditions that aided the surprise attack now hindered their advance. Additionally, the Allied forces regrouped quickly and managed to hold key defensive positions, preventing the Germans from achieving a swift victory.

The Battle of the Bulge was a pivotal moment in the war. The Allies responded with determination, utilizing air support and armored divisions to counter the German offensive. The heroic defense of Bastogne, a town in Belgium, by American troops became a symbol of Allied resistance. The Germans besieged the town, but the American forces, despite being surrounded and outnumbered, refused to surrender and held their ground until reinforcements arrived.

As the battle progressed, the weather improved, allowing the Allies to launch counterattacks. General George Patton's Third Army played a crucial role in breaking the encirclement and relieving the besieged Allied forces. The Germans' lack of resources and the encroaching Allied forces eventually forced them to retreat, and by January 1945, the bulge had been eliminated.

The Battle of the Bulge had significant consequences. While the Germans had hoped for a decisive victory, their defeat weakened their military strength and morale. The battle accelerated the momentum of the Allied advance into Germany, ultimately leading to the end of the war in Europe. The battle's lessons also highlighted the importance of intelligence, preparedness, and adaptability in warfare.

In conclusion, the Battle of the Bulge was a critical episode in World War II. The Germans' surprise attack created a bulge in the Allied lines, but determined resistance and unfavorable weather conditions slowed their advance. The battle showcased the resilience of the Allied forces and their ability to adapt to changing circumstances. Ultimately, the Allies managed to push back the Germans, marking a turning point in the war's favor and paving the way for the final victory over Nazi Germany.

Siege of Bastogne

The Siege of Bastogne, a critical episode in the larger Battle of the Bulge during World War II, stands as a testament to the resilience, determination, and heroism of both American and Allied forces. This pivotal battle took place from December 20 to December 27, 1944, in the town of Bastogne, Belgium. The German onslaught, launched as a surprise offensive in the Ardennes region, aimed to split the Allied lines and disrupt their advance. However, the defenders' unwavering resolve and the leadership of key figures turned the tide of the battle.

One of the key figures in the defense of Bastogne was Brigadier General Anthony McAuliffe, the acting commander of the 101st Airborne Division. When the German forces surrounded the town and demanded its surrender, McAuliffe famously replied with a resolute "Nuts!" This response captured the spirit of the defenders, who were determined to hold their ground against overwhelming odds.

The 101st Airborne Division, along with elements of the 10th Armored Division, became the focal point of the defense in Bastogne. Despite being outnumbered and encircled, they held their positions and fought back tenaciously against the German onslaught. The cold and harsh winter weather further added to the challenges faced by both sides, with freezing temperatures, heavy snowfall, and limited visibility impacting movement and operations.

The German forces, led by Field Marshal Gerd von Rundstedt and General Hasso von Manteuffel, aimed to quickly capture Bastogne and secure crucial roadways to pave the way for their advance. The Allies, caught off guard by the German offensive, initially struggled to respond effectively. The town of Bastogne held immense strategic importance, as its road network was essential for the movement of supplies and reinforcements.

The siege intensified as the German forces bombarded Bastogne with artillery fire and launched repeated attacks on the defenders' positions. The American and Allied troops, however, displayed exceptional bravery and resourcefulness, fending off the enemy's advances despite being surrounded and cut off from supply lines. The 101st Airborne Division's commander, Major General Maxwell D. Taylor, skillfully coordinated the defense efforts and facilitated the arrival of much-needed supplies and reinforcements through air drops.

As the siege continued, General George S. Patton's Third Army launched a daring counteroffensive to relieve the defenders in Bastogne. Despite the treacherous winter conditions, Patton's forces pushed through the German lines and successfully broke the encirclement. The arrival of Patton's forces provided a significant morale boost to the defenders and marked a turning point in the battle.

On December 26, 1944, the German forces finally recognized the futility of their efforts and withdrew from the outskirts of Bastogne. The siege was lifted, and the defenders emerged victorious. The battle showcased the courage and determination of the American and Allied troops, who stood strong against overwhelming odds and adverse weather conditions.

The Siege of Bastogne had far-reaching significance beyond its immediate outcome. The defenders' resilience and bravery bolstered the Allies' morale and highlighted their commitment to victory. The battle also marked a turning point in the larger Battle of the Bulge, weakening the German offensive and setting the stage for the eventual Allied counteroffensive that would lead to the liberation of Western Europe.

Battle of Berlin

In the waning days of World War II, the Battle of Berlin stood as the ultimate crescendo, a defining moment in the conflict that saw the warring nations converge upon the capital of Nazi Germany. As the year 1945 dawned, the world held its breath as the Soviet Red Army and the Allied forces advanced relentlessly, pushing towards Berlin to bring an end to the tyrannical regime of Adolf Hitler.

For Adolf Hitler and his crumbling Third Reich, Berlin became the last bastion of hope. The city had been fortified, and its defenders had been bolstered by fanatical Hitler Youth and elderly men, forming the Volkssturm, a last-ditch effort to defend their crumbling empire. Yet, despite their determination, they faced a formidable challenge in the combined might of the Soviet and Allied armies.

The battle commenced on April 16, 1945, with the Soviet Red Army launching a fierce offensive from the east. Facing desperate resistance, they fought street by street, pushing the Germans back towards the heart of the city. The iconic Brandenburg Gate became the emblematic symbol of the struggle, standing as both a physical and symbolic obstacle.

As the Soviet forces closed in, Adolf Hitler withdrew into his underground bunker, surrounded by loyal aides and generals. There, on April 30, 1945, he took his own life, leaving Grand Admiral Karl Dönitz to briefly lead the rapidly crumbling Third Reich. With Hitler's demise, the German forces lost their centralized leadership, adding to the chaos and disarray in Berlin.

On May 2, 1945, the Soviet forces captured the Reichstag, the seat of the German government, marking a significant turning point in the battle. The raising of the Soviet flag over the Reichstag became an iconic moment symbolizing the imminent defeat of Nazi Germany.

Meanwhile, from the west, the Allied forces, led by the United States, the United Kingdom, and France, continued their advance towards Berlin. However, they faced stiff resistance from the remaining German troops. The convergence of the Soviet and Allied forces set the stage for a climactic showdown to determine the fate of Berlin.

The final assault came to a head on May 7, 1945, when the German High Command surrendered unconditionally to the Allies, marking the end of the war in Europe. The next day, May 8, was designated as Victory in Europe Day (VE Day), a day of jubilation and relief for the people of Berlin and the world, as the long nightmare of war finally came to an end.

The Battle of Berlin left a profound impact on the city and its people. The destruction was devastating, with countless lives lost, and iconic landmarks reduced to rubble. The city was divided into East and West Berlin, becoming a microcosm of the larger Cold War between the Soviet Union and the Western Allies.

In conclusion, the Battle of Berlin was a pivotal moment in history that marked the end of World War II and the beginning of a new era. The resilience of the Soviet and Allied forces against the formidable German defenses in Berlin showcased the indomitable spirit of the human will. Today, Berlin stands as a testament to the horrors of war and the hope of peace, forever etched in the annals of history.

Hiroshima and Nagasaki

In August 1945, the world witnessed an event of unparalleled devastation that marked the culmination of World War II. The bombings of Hiroshima and Nagasaki, carried out by the United States, forever altered the course of history and demonstrated the immense destructive power of nuclear weapons.

On August 6, 1945, the city of Hiroshima became the target of the first atomic bomb ever deployed in warfare. Codenamed "Little Boy," this bomb was dropped by the American B-29 bomber named "Enola Gay." The explosion generated an immense release of energy, resulting in a blinding flash of light followed by a powerful shockwave and a mushroom cloud that billowed into the sky. The city's infrastructure was obliterated, and a vast area was engulfed in flames. Tens of thousands of lives were lost in an instant, and many more suffered from severe injuries and radiation exposure.

Just three days later, on August 9, 1945, the city of Nagasaki faced a similar fate. The atomic bomb named "Fat Man" was detonated over Nagasaki, releasing another wave of destruction. The city's industrial and residential areas were decimated, and thousands more lives were lost. The bombings of Hiroshima and Nagasaki marked a staggering display of the catastrophic consequences of nuclear warfare.

The immediate impact of the bombings was a devastating loss of life. In Hiroshima, it is estimated that between 90,000 and 166,000 people were killed in the immediate aftermath, while in Nagasaki, the death toll ranged from 39,000 to 80,000. The survivors, known as hibakusha, endured the physical and psychological scars of the bombings for the rest of their lives.

The bombings played a decisive role in bringing about the end of World War II. At the time, Japan was already facing significant military setbacks, and the bombings further eroded the nation's capacity to continue the war. The immense destruction and loss of life were stark reminders of the devastating potential of nuclear weapons. Faced with the reality of further destruction and the persistence of their enemies, Japan's leadership chose to surrender.

On August 15, 1945, Emperor Hirohito announced Japan's unconditional surrender, effectively ending the war. This momentous event is known as V-J Day (Victory over Japan Day). The bombings of Hiroshima and Nagasaki, tragic as they were, played a pivotal role in hastening the conclusion of the war and preventing further loss of life on both sides through a potentially prolonged invasion of Japan.

The bombings of Hiroshima and Nagasaki also initiated discussions about the ethical implications of using nuclear weapons and the moral responsibility of nations possessing such technology. The immense suffering and destruction caused by these bombings prompted efforts to prevent the future use of nuclear weapons and led to the establishment of arms control agreements and non-proliferation treaties.

In conclusion, the bombings of Hiroshima and Nagasaki were events of unprecedented devastation that signaled the end of World War II and demonstrated the catastrophic potential of nuclear weapons. The lives lost and the cities destroyed stand as enduring reminders of the need for international cooperation to prevent further use of such devastating weapons and to work towards a more peaceful and secure world.

Sinking of the Indianapolis

The mission of the USS Indianapolis and its subsequent sinking was a tragic and remarkable chapter of World War II. This naval vessel played a vital role in delivering a top-secret cargo that would contribute to the end of the war. However, its sinking and the harrowing experiences of the survivors highlighted the challenges and heroism of wartime at sea.

In July 1945, the USS Indianapolis embarked on a top-secret mission that would prove instrumental to the war effort. The ship carried components of the atomic bomb that would later be dropped on Hiroshima, Japan. The mission's purpose was to deliver this critical cargo to the Pacific island of Tinian, where the bomb would be assembled for its historic use.

Tragically, the USS Indianapolis was torpedoed by a Japanese submarine on July 30, 1945, just days after completing its mission. The ship sank rapidly, leaving many of its crew stranded in the shark-infested waters of the Pacific Ocean. Over 1,100 crew members faced a dire and life-threatening situation.

Survivors of the USS Indianapolis endured unimaginable hardships as they awaited rescue. Many of them found themselves adrift without lifeboats, exposed to the scorching sun, dehydration, and the constant threat of shark attacks. The survivors formed groups to support each other and tried to stay afloat using makeshift rafts and debris from the ship. Their ordeal was characterized by physical exhaustion, severe thirst, and a constant struggle to survive.

Remarkably, after days of uncertainty and suffering, the survivors were spotted by a routine patrol plane on August 2, 1945. A rescue operation was swiftly launched, and those who had endured days of torment were finally pulled from the water. The rescue process, however, was not without challenges, as many survivors were in critical condition due to exposure, injuries, and dehydration.

The sinking of the USS Indianapolis and the experiences of its survivors left a lasting impact. The tragedy highlighted the harsh realities of naval warfare and the sacrifices made by servicemen in the line of duty. The survivors' remarkable resilience and determination to survive showcased the strength of the human spirit in the face of extreme adversity.

The sinking of the USS Indianapolis also sparked controversy and discussions about the circumstances that led to the ship's demise and the delayed rescue. These discussions eventually led to changes in naval procedures and protocols to enhance the safety and security of naval vessels and their crews.

In conclusion, the mission of the USS Indianapolis and its sinking during World War II remains a somber and poignant episode in history. The ship's role in delivering crucial cargo for the atomic bomb demonstrated its significance to the war effort. The tragedy of its sinking and the subsequent survival of the crew underscored the challenges faced by servicemen at sea. The rescue of the survivors by a vigilant patrol plane serves as a testament to the dedication and bravery of those involved in wartime operations. The USS Indianapolis will forever be remembered as a vessel that carried both hope and tragedy, symbolizing the complex nature of war and the indomitable spirit of those who serve.

The Holocaust

The Holocaust stands as one of the most horrifying and tragic events in human history, forever marking the dark period of World War II. This systematic genocide orchestrated by the Nazi regime led by Adolf Hitler resulted in the mass murder of six million Jews, along with millions of others who were targeted due to their ethnicity, beliefs, disabilities, and political affiliations. The Holocaust left an indelible scar on the collective conscience of humanity and serves as a chilling reminder of the depths to which hatred and prejudice can lead.

The roots of the Holocaust can be traced back to the rise of Nazi ideology in the 1930s. Driven by anti-Semitic beliefs, Hitler's regime embarked on a campaign to marginalize, dehumanize, and persecute Jewish people in Europe. This campaign began with discriminatory laws that restricted the rights of Jews, and over time escalated to forced segregation, violent pogroms, and eventually mass murder.

The systematic implementation of the Holocaust took various forms, each more horrifying than the last. Jewish communities were stripped of their property, businesses, and rights. Ghettos were established to isolate and control Jewish populations, subjecting them to appalling living conditions, malnutrition, and disease. As the Nazi regime expanded its conquests, it created death camps equipped with gas chambers and crematoria, where victims were exterminated in unimaginable numbers.

One of the most infamous death camps was Auschwitz-Birkenau, where an estimated 1.1 million people, the majority of them Jews, were murdered. The horrors of Auschwitz, along with other camps like Treblinka and Sobibor, symbolize the depths of human cruelty and the deliberate dehumanization of individuals based on their identity.

The Holocaust was not limited to Jews alone. The Nazi regime also targeted other groups, including Romani people, disabled individuals, political dissidents, and those who resisted the regime. The systematic nature of the genocide extended to the Einsatzgruppen, mobile killing squads that roamed Eastern Europe, murdering people in mass shootings.

The significance of the Holocaust extends far beyond the staggering number of lives lost. It serves as a stark reminder of the consequences of unchecked hatred, bigotry, and intolerance. The Holocaust also underscores the importance of remembrance, education, and vigilance in preventing such atrocities from happening again.

In the aftermath of World War II, the world began to grapple with the enormity of the Holocaust. The Nuremberg Trials held those responsible for war crimes accountable, but the scars left behind were deeper and more profound. Survivors faced the challenge of rebuilding their lives, while societies struggled to come to terms with the atrocities that had taken place.

The memory of the Holocaust has led to efforts to ensure that the world never forgets. Holocaust museums, memorials, and educational programs have been established worldwide to honor the victims, bear witness to their suffering, and teach future generations about the dangers of hatred and prejudice. The phrase "Never Again" has become a rallying cry against genocide and human rights abuses.

The Holocaust remains a harrowing testament to the depths of human cruelty and the consequences of unchecked hatred. The systematic genocide orchestrated by the Nazi regime during World War II led to the murder of millions of innocent lives. The Holocaust serves as a haunting reminder of the importance of combating intolerance, upholding human rights, and fostering a world where such atrocities can never happen again.

The Final Solution

The "Final Solution" stands as a dark chapter in human history, representing the systematic and genocidal plan devised by Nazi Germany during World War II to annihilate the Jewish people. Emerging as a culmination of Adolf Hitler's anti-Semitic ideology and the Nazis' pursuit of racial purity, the Final Solution resulted in the Holocaust, a horrific genocide that claimed the lives of millions of innocent individuals.

The origins of the Final Solution can be traced to Hitler's virulent anti-Semitism, as outlined in his infamous book, "Mein Kampf." The Nazis, under Hitler's leadership, propagated the idea of an Aryan master race and sought the elimination of perceived racial enemies, particularly Jews, whom they falsely scapegoated for Germany's perceived woes.

The implementation of the Final Solution unfolded in stages, evolving from discriminatory laws and policies to mass extermination. The initial phase involved anti-Jewish legislation, such as the Nuremberg Laws of 1935, which stripped Jews of their citizenship and prohibited intermarriage with non-Jews. As the war progressed, the persecution escalated with violent pogroms, Kristallnacht (Night of Broken Glass) in 1938, and the establishment of ghettos to segregate and exploit Jewish communities.

However, it was during the Wannsee Conference in January 1942 that the Nazi leadership formalized the Final Solution. Led by SS-Obergruppenführer Reinhard Heydrich, high-ranking officials gathered to coordinate the mass extermination of European Jews. The decision to systematically annihilate entire Jewish populations through mass shootings and later, extermination camps, marked the horrifying realization of the Final Solution.

Extermination camps, such as Auschwitz, Sobibor, and Treblinka, became sites of unparalleled brutality. The Nazis implemented a ruthless and efficient process, employing gas chambers and crematoria to systematically murder millions of men, women, and children. Victims were often deceived into thinking they were being resettled or subjected to forced labor, only to face mass extermination upon arrival.

The Holocaust unfolded on an unprecedented scale, leading to the genocide of six million Jews, along with millions of others deemed undesirable by the Nazis, including Romani people, disabled individuals, and political dissidents. The Final Solution extended beyond Germany's borders, with the Nazis orchestrating the mass murder of Jews across German-occupied territories in Eastern and Western Europe.

The aftermath of the Holocaust left a devastating impact on survivors, families, and the collective memory of humanity. Liberating Allied forces encountered emaciated survivors, evidence of mass graves, and the sheer horror of the extermination camps. The Nuremberg Trials sought to hold key Nazi officials accountable for crimes against humanity, including the implementation of the Final Solution.

The Final Solution remains a haunting reminder of the atrocities committed during the Holocaust and the depths of human depravity. It stands as a testament to the dangers of unchecked hatred, discrimination, and the consequences of extremist ideologies. The international community, in the aftermath of World War II, committed to the principle of "Never Again," emphasizing the need to prevent genocidal acts and protect human rights.

In conclusion, the Final Solution represents the calculated and genocidal plan devised by Nazi Germany to exterminate the Jewish people during World War II. This dark chapter in history unfolded through discriminatory laws, violent persecution, and the establishment of extermination camps. The Holocaust, resulting from the Final Solution, stands as an indelible symbol of the horrors of genocide, emphasizing the importance of remembrance, education, and the prevention of future atrocities.

Kristallnacht

Kristallnacht, also known as the Night of Broken Glass, stands as a chilling and pivotal event in the lead-up to the Holocaust, marking a turning point in Nazi Germany's persecution of Jews. Occurring on November 9-10, 1938, Kristallnacht was a coordinated series of violent attacks against Jewish individuals, businesses, synagogues, and homes throughout Germany and Austria. The aftermath left streets strewn with shattered glass from vandalized storefronts, hence the name "Night of Broken Glass."

The pretext for Kristallnacht was the assassination of German diplomat Ernst vom Rath by Herschel Grynszpan, a young Polish Jew, in Paris. The Nazi regime exploited this tragic event to unleash a wave of anti-Semitic violence. Nazi officials and members of the SA (Sturmabteilung) and SS (Schutzstaffel) orchestrated the widespread destruction, with orders not to intervene or protect Jewish property.

The violence unfolded across cities, towns, and villages, targeting Jewish-owned businesses, homes, and synagogues. Thousands of storefronts were smashed, looted, and set ablaze. Jewish homes were ransacked, and countless Jews were physically assaulted, humiliated, or arrested. Synagogues, the spiritual centers of Jewish communities, became particular targets. Approximately 267 synagogues were destroyed, many set on fire, and Jewish prayer books and Torah scrolls were desecrated.

The name Kristallnacht itself reflects the extensive use of broken glass during the attacks, symbolizing the destruction and devastation wrought upon the Jewish community. The violence was not only physical but also psychological, as the terror instilled fear and despair among Jewish individuals and families.

In addition to the immediate physical harm and destruction, Kristallnacht had broader and more insidious implications. The event marked a clear escalation in the Nazi regime's anti-

Semitic policies. The violence was not only condoned but actively encouraged by the government, signaling the official endorsement of state-sponsored anti-Semitism. The destruction of synagogues and Jewish businesses served as a prelude to more systematic measures that would follow, including discriminatory laws, forced deportations, and eventually the implementation of the "Final Solution."

Kristallnacht also had profound international ramifications. The brutality of the attacks shocked the world and prompted condemnation from some governments and individuals. However, it also exposed the reluctance of many nations to intervene or alter their policies towards refugees fleeing Nazi persecution. The international response, or lack thereof, highlighted the challenges of confronting the rising Nazi threat and the deep-rooted anti-Semitism prevalent in various parts of the world.

In the aftermath of Kristallnacht, the Nazi regime imposed fines on the Jewish community for the damages incurred during the attacks. Jewish businesses faced additional taxes, and restrictions intensified, further isolating and marginalizing the Jewish population. The violence of Kristallnacht served as a foreboding precursor to the horrors of the Holocaust, underscoring the urgency of addressing the plight of Jews under Nazi rule.

In conclusion, Kristallnacht remains a haunting chapter in the history of Nazi Germany and the Holocaust. The orchestrated violence, destruction of synagogues, and widespread terror inflicted upon Jewish communities marked a watershed moment, signaling a dark path toward systemic persecution and mass atrocities. The scars of Kristallnacht lingered as a grim foreshadowing of the immense human tragedy that would unfold in the years to come, underscoring the importance of remembering and learning from such harrowing events in our collective history.

The Zegota

During the harrowing years of World War II and the Holocaust, an underground organization known as Zegota emerged as a beacon of hope for those persecuted under Nazi rule. Zegota, a Polish Council to Aid Jews, dedicated its efforts to providing assistance and protection to Jewish people facing unimaginable horrors during the Holocaust. With bravery and compassion, Zegota played a crucial role in saving countless lives and became a symbol of resistance against the Nazi regime.

Formed in December 1942 in Warsaw, Poland, Zegota was a response to the relentless persecution and extermination of Jews by the occupying Nazi forces. Comprising individuals from various backgrounds, including activists, intellectuals, and religious leaders, Zegota was a remarkable example of unity and solidarity in the face of unspeakable evil.

Zegota's primary mission was to rescue and support Jewish individuals trapped in the ghettos and hiding from Nazi persecution. The organization established a network of safe houses and secret routes to smuggle Jews out of ghettos and to find them shelter with non-Jewish families or in convents and monasteries.

To protect Jewish children, who were particularly vulnerable during the Holocaust, Zegota organized efforts to find new homes and families willing to provide them with shelter and safety. These courageous acts of resistance saved numerous Jewish children from the fate of the concentration camps and offered them a chance at survival.

In addition to rescuing Jews, Zegota also provided financial aid, forged identification documents, and distributed food and medical supplies to those in need. They worked tirelessly to help Jews escape from the Nazis' clutches and to provide them with the support necessary for survival.

Zegota operated under the constant threat of discovery by the Nazi authorities. If caught, its members faced certain death. However, their unwavering commitment to the cause of saving innocent lives pushed them to continue their brave efforts despite the risks.

Their determination and courage in the face of danger earned Zegota the distinction of being one of the few organized rescue movements during the Holocaust. The members of Zegota knew that their actions were essential in countering the brutal Nazi regime and providing hope and assistance to those who had lost everything.

As the war raged on, Zegota's influence and operations expanded beyond Warsaw, spreading its network across various Polish cities. Their acts of defiance and humanity reached beyond borders, saving Jewish lives throughout occupied Europe.

After the war, many Zegota members faced trials and persecution from the communist regime that followed in Poland. Nevertheless, their legacy remained an inspiration to generations, and their heroic deeds were recognized and honored worldwide.

In conclusion, Zegota, the Polish Council to Aid Jews, stands as a testament to human compassion and courage during the darkest hours of the Holocaust. By risking their lives to save countless Jewish individuals from the clutches of the Nazi regime, Zegota became a symbol of resistance, hope, and humanity in a time of unimaginable evil. human life.

Irena Sendler

In the dark and horrifying times of the Holocaust during World War II, one woman's bravery and compassion shone like a beacon of hope. Irena Sendler, a Polish social worker, risked her life to save the lives of Jewish children from the clutches of Nazi persecution. Her courageous efforts and selflessness left an indelible mark on history, earning her the title of a righteous gentile and a symbol of humanity's triumph over evil.

Born in 1910 in Otwock, Poland, Irena Sendler grew up with a strong sense of social justice and empathy for those facing adversity. As the Holocaust unfolded, she witnessed the horrors inflicted upon the Jewish community under Nazi occupation. Determined to make a difference, she joined an underground resistance network known as Żegota, dedicated to aiding Jews and other persecuted groups.

Irena Sendler's primary mission was to rescue Jewish children from the Warsaw Ghetto, where thousands of Jews were forced to live in deplorable conditions. She risked her life daily, posing as a nurse and social worker, to gain access to the ghetto. Once inside, she orchestrated a covert operation to smuggle out as many children as possible, often hiding them in bags, suitcases, or coffins to avoid detection.

Irena and her network of brave collaborators provided the rescued children with false identities and placed them with non-Jewish families or in orphanages. These acts of resistance and rescue not only saved the children from certain death but also gave them a chance at a new life, free from the horrors of the Holocaust.

In 1943, Irena Sendler's heroic efforts came to the attention of the Gestapo, and she was arrested and brutally tortured. Despite the excruciating pain and danger, she refused to betray her network or the children she had saved. Her captors sentenced her to death, but fellow members of the resistance bribed a German guard to spare her life. Even facing imminent execution, Irena never lost her resolve or revealed any vital information.

After her miraculous escape, Irena continued her work in secret, never seeking recognition or glory. Sadly, the war ended, but many of the children she saved were unable to reunite with their families due to the scale of devastation caused by the Holocaust. Irena meticulously recorded the identities of the rescued children in jars, which she buried under a tree in hopes of reuniting them with their families after the war. Tragically, most of the children's families did not survive, but her efforts left a lasting testament to her dedication and love for humanity.

Decades later, Irena Sendler's extraordinary story of courage and compassion came to light, and she received international recognition for her selfless deeds. She was honored with numerous awards, including the prestigious Righteous Among the Nations designation by Yad Vashem, Israel's Holocaust remembrance center.

Irena Sendler passed away in 2008, but her legacy lives on as a symbol of hope and humanity's triumph over evil. Her bravery in the face of unimaginable horrors continues to inspire generations to stand up against injustice and never forget the power of compassion and selflessness in times of darkness. Her actions serve as a timeless reminder that even in the darkest moments of history, ordinary individuals can make an extraordinary difference through acts of kindness and courage.

Anne Frank

Anne Frank was a Jewish girl who lived during one of the darkest periods of human history, World War II. Born on June 12, 1929, in Frankfurt, Germany, she became a symbol of hope, resilience, and the human spirit in the face of adversity. Anne's life, though tragically cut short, continues to inspire people around the world.

Anne's family fled Germany in 1933 when Adolf Hitler's rise to power made life increasingly dangerous for Jewish people. They settled in Amsterdam, Netherlands, hoping for safety and a fresh start. However, their hopes were shattered when Germany invaded the Netherlands in 1940, plunging the country into the horrors of Nazi occupation.

As anti-Jewish measures intensified, the Franks faced discrimination and persecution. To escape the Nazis' reach, Anne's family, along with another Jewish family, went into hiding in a secret annex above her father's business premises. The hiding place, concealed behind a movable bookcase, became their sanctuary from the atrocities outside.

During their two years in hiding, Anne kept a diary, which she received as a birthday present on her thirteenth birthday. In her diary, she poured out her thoughts, feelings, and reflections on life in confinement. Through her words, readers glimpse the inner world of a young girl grappling with the turmoil of adolescence amidst the backdrop of war.

Anne's diary is a poignant testament to the human spirit's resilience in the face of adversity. Despite the confinement and fear, she maintained her optimism and belief in the goodness of people. Her unwavering spirit shines through her writings, offering solace and inspiration to generations.

Tragically, the Franks' hiding place was betrayed, and on August 4, 1944, they were arrested by the Gestapo, the Nazi secret police. Anne and her family were deported to concentration camps, where they endured unimaginable suffering. Anne, along with her sister Margot, was later transferred to the Bergen-Belsen concentration camp, where they both perished from typhus in early 1945, just weeks before the camp's liberation.

After the war, Anne's father, Otto Frank, the sole survivor of the family, returned to Amsterdam and was given Anne's diary by Miep Gies, one of the brave individuals who helped hide them. Recognizing the significance of his daughter's writings, Otto made it his mission to fulfill Anne's wish of becoming a published writer.

Anne's diary, titled "The Diary of a Young Girl" or "Anne Frank: The Diary of a Young Girl," was published in 1947. Translated into numerous languages, it has become one of the most widely read books in the world. Through her diary, Anne's voice continues to resonate, offering insights into the human experience and reminding us of the importance of empathy, tolerance, and the enduring power of hope.

Anne Frank's legacy transcends time and borders. Her story serves as a poignant reminder of the consequences of hatred and bigotry, urging us to confront injustice and strive for a world where tolerance, understanding, and compassion prevail. In her own words, she remains a beacon of hope: "Despite everything, I believe that people are really good at heart."

Auschwitz

Auschwitz, located in the town of Oswiecim in southern Poland, was one of the most infamous prison camps established by Nazi Germany during World War II. It consisted of three main camps: Auschwitz I (the original camp), Auschwitz II-Birkenau (the extermination camp), and Auschwitz III-Monowitz (a labor camp). The camp was constructed in 1940 and became a central site for the Holocaust, where millions of innocent people, primarily Jews, were systematically exterminated.

Auschwitz I, the administrative center, was initially built to house Polish political prisoners. The camp's design was deliberately bleak, with rows of brick barracks surrounded by electrified barbed wire fences and watchtowers. Prisoners lived in overcrowded and unsanitary conditions, enduring extreme hardship and deplorable treatment.

Daily life in Auschwitz was a harrowing ordeal for the prisoners. They faced backbreaking forced labor, meager rations, and brutal punishments at the hands of the SS guards. The prisoners were subjected to constant fear and uncertainty, never knowing if they would be selected for death in the gas chambers.

Auschwitz II-Birkenau, the largest of the three camps, was primarily designed as an extermination camp. Its layout included vast gas chambers and crematoria, where trains packed with victims arrived regularly. Upon arrival, prisoners were subjected to a selection process, where SS doctors determined who was fit for forced labor and who would be sent to the gas chambers. The extermination process was an efficient and cold-hearted operation, tragically ending the lives of countless innocent men, women, and children.

The Auschwitz III-Monowitz camp, also known as Buna-Monowitz, was established to exploit forced labor for the German chemical company IG Farben. Prisoners worked in harsh conditions, producing synthetic rubber and other chemicals vital to the Nazi war effort.

Auschwitz was a place of immense suffering, cruelty, and death. The camp's horrific legacy has become a symbol of the Holocaust, where over one million innocent lives were lost, making it one of the most tragic chapters in human history.

Liberation of Auschwitz by the Soviet Army in January 1945 marked the end of the camp's operation. Today, Auschwitz stands as a memorial and museum, dedicated to preserving the memory of those who perished and educating the world about the horrors of the Holocaust. It serves as a solemn reminder of the atrocities committed during World War II, urging humanity to never forget and to strive for a world free from hatred and prejudice.

Daily Life in Auschwitz

Daily life in Auschwitz for prisoners was a harrowing ordeal, marked by relentless brutality, dehumanization, and the constant struggle for survival. Drawing from prisoner accounts, it is possible to glimpse into the grim reality that unfolded within the confines of this notorious concentration and extermination camp during the Holocaust.

For those incarcerated in Auschwitz, the day often began with the dreaded early morning roll call, an assembly that took place in all weather conditions. Prisoners were forced to stand for hours, enduring the harsh elements while SS officers meticulously counted each inmate. Any deviation from the required posture or any sign of weakness resulted in severe punishment, further instilling a sense of fear and submission.

Food scarcity was a defining feature of daily life in Auschwitz. Meals were meager and nutritionally deficient, consisting of watery soup, a small piece of bread, and occasionally a morsel of margarine. The inadequate rations left prisoners emaciated, weakened, and susceptible to various diseases that thrived in the unsanitary conditions of the camp.

Work assignments were a central aspect of daily life, with prisoners subjected to grueling labor in various capacities. Whether forced into construction projects, agricultural work, or other physically demanding tasks, inmates toiled under the watchful eyes of SS guards. Exhaustion, malnutrition, and the absence of proper clothing made the daily work regimen a torturous experience for prisoners, many of whom faced the constant threat of physical abuse.

Auschwitz was notorious for its medical experiments, and prisoners were subjected to inhumane and often lethal procedures. Those targeted for experiments endured unimaginable pain, and many did not survive the sadistic curiosity of the Nazi doctors. The infamous Dr. Josef Mengele, known as the "Angel of Death," conducted gruesome experiments on twins and individuals with physical abnormalities, adding an extra layer of horror to the daily existence of prisoners.

Living conditions in the overcrowded barracks were deplorable. Inmates were crammed into tight quarters with minimal hygiene facilities. The lack of sanitation and the pervasive presence of lice and disease contributed to the rapid spread of infections. The barracks offered little respite from the harsh realities of daily life, providing only a grim and cramped space for prisoners to sleep, if sleep could be achieved amidst the anguish and despair.

Daily life in Auschwitz was also marked by the constant specter of death. Mass shootings, hangings, and the use of gas chambers for mass extermination were chillingly routine occurrences. The fear of being selected for immediate extermination cast a perpetual shadow over prisoners, who lived with the ever-present awareness that their lives could be extinguished at any moment.

Prisoners in Auschwitz formed a complex social fabric, with various nationalities and ethnicities coexisting under the harshest of circumstances. Solidarity among inmates became a source of support and resistance against the oppressors. Acts of kindness, sharing of meager resources, and a collective will to survive were essential elements of the prisoner community's daily struggle.

Surviving Auschwitz required not only physical resilience but also mental strength. Prisoners clung to the hope of liberation, relying on each other for emotional support. Despite the overwhelming odds stacked against them, some managed to maintain a semblance of humanity and dignity amid the dehumanizing conditions.

In conclusion, daily life in Auschwitz was a nightmarish existence, characterized by deprivation, forced labor, medical experiments, and the constant threat of death.

Liberation of Auschwitz

The Liberation of Auschwitz, a pivotal moment in the history of the Holocaust, marked the end of the horrific atrocities committed within the confines of the notorious Auschwitz concentration and extermination camp. From the Jewish prisoners' perspective, the liberation symbolized a glimmer of hope, an end to unimaginable suffering, and the beginning of a journey toward healing and rebuilding their shattered lives. Simultaneously, for the liberators, it was a moment of confronting the incomprehensible cruelty and the responsibility to bring justice to those who had endured indescribable horrors.

For the Jewish prisoners who survived the brutal conditions at Auschwitz, the liberation was an unexpected and emotional reprieve. As Allied forces advanced through Europe, the walls of Auschwitz bore witness to years of dehumanization, mass murders, and unspeakable experiments. The arrival of liberating forces signaled the end of their nightmare, offering a chance to reclaim their humanity and rebuild their lives.

Survivors of Auschwitz recount the overwhelming mix of emotions during liberation. There was disbelief that freedom was finally within reach, coupled with the haunting memories of lost family members, friends, and the indelible scars of the Holocaust. Liberation brought a mixture of relief, sorrow, and the daunting task of coming to terms with the trauma endured within the camp's barbed wire confines.

From the perspective of the liberators, the scenes they encountered at Auschwitz were beyond comprehension. Allied soldiers, many of whom were unaware of the full extent of the Holocaust, were confronted with the stark reality of the genocide perpetrated by the Nazis. The sight of emaciated and traumatized survivors, along with the evidence of mass extermination in the form of piles of corpses, gas chambers, and crematoria, left an indelible mark on the liberators.

For the soldiers liberating Auschwitz, the immediate priority was to provide aid and comfort to the survivors. Medical care, food, and attempts to restore a sense of humanity were paramount. The liberators, often overwhelmed by the scale of the atrocities, faced the challenging task of understanding the depths of human suffering and ensuring that justice would be served.

Both Jewish survivors and liberators grappled with the magnitude of the Holocaust's impact. The survivors faced the arduous process of rebuilding their lives, haunted by the memories of Auschwitz. Many sought to bear witness to the atrocities they had experienced, sharing their stories to ensure that the world would never forget the horrors of the Holocaust.

The liberators, on the other hand, were entrusted with the responsibility of holding the perpetrators accountable. The discovery of Auschwitz's horrors fueled international outrage and a commitment to seeking justice for the victims. War crimes trials, including the Nuremberg Trials, became a means to confront the perpetrators and establish a historical record of the atrocities committed during the Holocaust.

The Liberation of Auschwitz remains a somber chapter in history, marked by the resilience of survivors and the realization of the world's obligation to remember and learn from the atrocities of the past. From the Jewish perspective, liberation represented the triumph of the human spirit over unimaginable adversity. For the liberators, it was an awakening to the brutal realities of the Holocaust and a commitment to ensuring that such horrors would never be repeated. Together, the survivors and liberators bear witness to the enduring importance of remembrance, education, and the pursuit of justice in preventing the recurrence of such dark chapters in human history.

Importance of Remembering Auschwitz

Preserving and remembering Auschwitz is of paramount importance to the Jewish people and the world at large, serving as a solemn obligation to honor the memory of the victims, educate future generations, and prevent the recurrence of such atrocities. Auschwitz, synonymous with the horrors of the Holocaust, stands as a haunting symbol of the depths humanity can descend to when fueled by hatred and prejudice.

For the Jewish people, Auschwitz holds a unique and poignant significance. It stands as a tangible reminder of the immense suffering endured by millions of Jews during the Holocaust. The preservation of Auschwitz is a testament to the resilience of Jewish survivors who, against all odds, emerged from the darkest chapter in history to rebuild their lives and communities. The site encapsulates the collective memory of a people who faced extermination but ultimately triumphed over the forces of hatred.

Auschwitz, with its barracks, gas chambers, and remnants of systematic genocide, represents the magnitude of the Holocaust's impact on Jewish history. It serves as a sacred space for reflection, mourning, and remembrance, allowing successive generations to connect with the profound sacrifices made by their ancestors. Preserving Auschwitz ensures that the stories of the victims are not consigned to oblivion, but rather etched into the collective consciousness of Jewish identity.

Beyond the Jewish community, Auschwitz holds global significance as a stark reminder of the consequences of intolerance and indifference. The preservation of Auschwitz is a commitment to upholding the principles of human rights, justice, and the inherent dignity of every individual. The world must confront the painful truths embedded in Auschwitz to understand the importance of fostering tolerance, empathy, and a shared responsibility to prevent hatred from gaining a foothold.

Educating future generations about Auschwitz is a crucial step in preventing the recurrence of genocidal atrocities. The preserved site serves as a powerful educational tool, allowing visitors to witness firsthand the horrors of the Holocaust. The authenticity of Auschwitz compels individuals to confront uncomfortable truths, fostering a commitment to human rights and the rejection of prejudice in all its forms.

The preservation of Auschwitz also serves as a moral imperative for the world to actively combat denial and revisionism. Holocaust denial is a sinister distortion of historical reality that seeks to undermine the truth and diminish the gravity of the atrocities committed. By preserving Auschwitz, the world sends a resounding message that the undeniable evidence of the Holocaust must be upheld, and its memory safeguarded against those who seek to distort or erase it.

Moreover, Auschwitz stands as a call to action against contemporary manifestations of hatred and discrimination. In a world where prejudice and intolerance persist, Auschwitz compels us to be vigilant guardians of human rights. It challenges societies to confront hate speech, bigotry, and discrimination in all its forms, ensuring that the lessons of the past guide us toward a more just and compassionate future.

In conclusion, the preservation and remembrance of Auschwitz are paramount for the Jewish people and the world. It is a sacred duty to honor the memory of the victims, educate future generations, and fortify the collective commitment to human rights and tolerance. Auschwitz stands not only as a memorial to the past but as a beacon urging humanity to reject hatred and prejudice, fostering a world where the atrocities of the Holocaust remain inconceivable.

The Liberation of the Nazi Death Train

During the waning days of World War II, as the Allied forces advanced into German territory, a chilling revelation came to light—the existence of the Nazi "Death Train." This macabre moniker encapsulated a train, discovered by advancing American forces in April 1945, that carried thousands of emaciated and desperate prisoners who had survived the horrors of concentration camps. The rescue of these survivors stands as a testament to both the atrocities committed during the Holocaust and the humanity that prevailed in the face of such darkness.

The Nazi "Death Train" was a ghastly manifestation of the genocidal intent of the Third Reich. As the Allies closed in, the Nazis sought to erase evidence of their heinous crimes by transporting concentration camp prisoners away from the advancing front lines. Packed into overcrowded and unsanitary conditions, the prisoners were subjected to unimaginable suffering during the journey. Hunger, disease, and exhaustion were their constant companions, and many did not survive the brutal ordeal.

The discovery of the train by American forces, specifically the 743rd Tank Battalion of the U.S. Army, occurred near the town of Farsleben in central Germany. The stark reality that unfolded before the liberators was one of horror and disbelief. The emaciated bodies of survivors, clad in the tattered remnants of striped concentration camp uniforms, spoke volumes about the unimaginable conditions they had endured.

The rescue operation that ensued was a race against time to provide medical care, sustenance, and comfort to those who had been subjected to the depths of human cruelty. American soldiers, confronted with the harrowing scenes before them, responded with compassion and a determination to alleviate the suffering of the survivors. Medics worked tirelessly to attend to the immediate medical needs of the prisoners, offering a glimmer of hope to those who had faced the specter of death on the "Death Train."

As the survivors began to comprehend their liberation, gratitude mixed with disbelief. The reality of their newfound freedom, juxtaposed against the grim memories of the concentration camps, created a complex emotional landscape. The "Death Train" had brought them to the brink of annihilation, but the arrival of the American forces signaled a turning point in their fate.

The rescue of the prisoners from the Nazi "Death Train" symbolizes the triumph of humanity over the darkest forces of history. In the face of the Holocaust's unimaginable horrors, the Allied forces, and particularly the American soldiers involved in the liberation, demonstrated a commitment to justice and compassion. The survivors, although physically and emotionally scarred, were given a chance to rebuild their lives, free from the shackles of oppression.

The aftermath of the rescue saw the survivors receiving essential care, including medical treatment, nourishment, and the support needed to begin the process of healing. The liberated prisoners, once marked for extermination, became witnesses to history, living testaments to the resilience of the human spirit and the enduring pursuit of justice.

The Nazi "Death Train" and its rescue by American forces serve as a stark reminder of the atrocities committed during the Holocaust. The train's grim cargo and the subsequent acts of compassion and liberation underscore the importance of remembering the darkest chapters of history to prevent such horrors from being repeated. In the face of profound darkness, the rescue of the survivors on the "Death Train" stands as a beacon of hope, symbolizing the triumph of humanity over the depths of inhumanity.

The Warsaw Zoo

The Warsaw Zoo, located in Poland's capital city, holds a unique and poignant place in history, especially during the Holocaust. Before World War II, the Warsaw Zoo, established in 1928 by Jan and Antonina Żabiński, was a thriving institution known for its diverse collection of animals and beautiful gardens. However, as the Nazi occupation of Poland unfolded, the zoo's story took a remarkable turn, becoming a haven for Jewish individuals seeking refuge from persecution.

When Germany invaded Poland in 1939, the Warsaw Zoo suffered immense damage. Many of its animals were killed, and the infrastructure was severely affected. Despite these challenges, Jan and Antonina Żabiński, the zookeepers, demonstrated immense courage and compassion. They decided to use their zoo as a hiding place for Jews escaping the brutal persecution of the Nazis.

The Żabiński family transformed the zoo into a clandestine refuge, providing shelter to Jews and resistance fighters. The zoo's destroyed animal enclosures became hiding spots for those seeking safety. Underground tunnels, cages, and hidden compartments within the zoo's buildings were ingeniously used to conceal people from the watchful eyes of the occupying forces.

Antonina Żabińska played a pivotal role in this clandestine operation. She developed a special bond with the hidden individuals, treating them as guests rather than refugees. Her compassionate and nurturing approach helped alleviate the constant fear and stress faced by those seeking refuge at the zoo. Antonina's ability to navigate through the dangerous landscape of Nazi-occupied Warsaw contributed significantly to the success of the operation.

Jan Żabiński, in addition to managing the zoo, actively participated in the Polish resistance against the Nazis. The Warsaw Zoo served as a hub for the Home Army, and Jan used his position to gather intelligence, helping the resistance in its efforts against the occupation. The zookeepers' dual roles – as rescuers of Jews and as resistance members – showcased their commitment to opposing Nazi oppression on multiple fronts.

The Żabiński family's courageous efforts resulted in saving the lives of over 300 Jews during the Holocaust. The zoo became a place of hope and survival, defying the grim reality of the surrounding city. Among those sheltered at the Warsaw Zoo were men, women, and children who, thanks to the Żabińskis, managed to escape the brutality of the Holocaust and its devastating consequences.

The Warsaw Zoo's role in saving Jewish lives remained relatively unknown for many years after the war. It wasn't until the publication of Diane Ackerman's book "The Zookeeper's Wife" in 2007 that the world learned about the extraordinary acts of bravery carried out by the Żabiński family. The book brought international attention to their story, highlighting the significance of the Warsaw Zoo as a symbol of resilience and humanity during one of history's darkest periods.

In 1968, the Żabiński family was honored by the Yad Vashem Holocaust Memorial in Jerusalem as Righteous Among the Nations, recognizing their heroic actions in saving Jewish lives during the Holocaust. The Warsaw Zoo, once a place of entertainment and education, became a living testament to the triumph of compassion and bravery over hatred and persecution. The legacy of the Warsaw Zoo and the Żabiński family stands as a beacon of hope, reminding us of the capacity for goodness even in the darkest times.

V-E Day

V-E Day, short for "Victory in Europe Day," is a momentous historical event that signifies the end of World War II in Europe. This day, celebrated on May 8, 1945, marked a turning point in global history, bringing an end to years of devastating conflict, immense loss of life, and widespread destruction across the European continent. V-E Day was met with exuberant celebrations, relief, and a sense of hope for a brighter future.

Throughout the 1940s, the world was embroiled in a massive conflict known as World War II. Nazi Germany, under the leadership of Adolf Hitler, had expanded its influence and aggression across Europe, leading to a brutal occupation of many countries. The Allied forces, including countries such as the United States, the United Kingdom, the Soviet Union, and others, united to combat this menace and bring an end to the Axis powers' aggression.

V-E Day was the culmination of years of intense fighting, strategic planning, and the collective efforts of the Allied forces. The relentless campaigns and battles on various fronts had finally resulted in the weakening of Nazi Germany's military and economic capabilities. As the Allied forces advanced into Germany from different directions, the situation for the Axis powers became increasingly dire.

The turning point that led to V-E Day was the unconditional surrender of Nazi Germany. Adolf Hitler's suicide on April 30, 1945, followed by the fall of Berlin to the Soviet forces, signaled the imminent collapse of the Nazi regime. On May 7, 1945, the German armed forces officially surrendered to the Allies, and the surrender became effective on May 8, 1945, which was designated as V-E Day.

The news of Germany's surrender was met with an outpouring of joy, relief, and celebration across Europe and around the world. In London, crowds thronged the streets, waving flags, singing, and dancing in a display of unbridled jubilation.

People hugged each other, tears streaming down their faces, as they celebrated the end of a conflict that had brought so much suffering.

V-E Day marked the beginning of a new chapter for Europe and the world. It was a moment of shared victory and unity, a testament to the power of international cooperation and the resilience of humanity in the face of adversity. However, the celebrations were also tempered by the recognition of the immense human cost of the war and the need for rebuilding and recovery.

The aftermath of V-E Day saw Europe emerge from the shadows of war and embark on a journey of reconstruction. Cities, towns, and infrastructure that had been ravaged by the conflict were gradually rebuilt. Amid the physical reconstruction, nations also grappled with the psychological and emotional scars left by the war, striving to create a more stable and peaceful future.

V-E Day's significance extended beyond the immediate celebration. It marked the beginning of a complex period of post-war diplomacy, negotiations, and the establishment of new alliances. The formation of the United Nations and the recognition of the need for international cooperation aimed at preventing future conflicts were among the outcomes of this pivotal time in history.

V-J Day

V-J Day, short for "Victory over Japan Day," marks a significant moment in history that commemorates the end of World War II and the official surrender of Japan to the Allied forces on September 2, 1945. This momentous event brought an end to years of global conflict and marked the final defeat of the Axis powers, including Japan. The declaration of V-J Day was met with immense relief, celebration, and a sense of hope for a more peaceful world.

During the early 1940s, the world was engulfed in a devastating war that had resulted in tremendous loss of life, economic turmoil, and widespread destruction. The war effort was a united endeavor by the Allied forces, including countries such as the United States, the United Kingdom, the Soviet Union, and others. Japan, a key Axis power, had been engaged in a prolonged conflict, which had inflicted suffering on both military personnel and civilian populations.

The turning point that eventually led to V-J Day was the dropping of atomic bombs on the Japanese cities of Hiroshima and Nagasaki in August 1945. These bombings had a catastrophic impact, causing extensive loss of life and devastating damage. Realizing the dire situation and recognizing the futility of further resistance, Japan's leaders made the momentous decision to surrender.

On September 2, 1945, aboard the USS Missouri in Tokyo Bay, Japanese officials signed the Instrument of Surrender, effectively ending the war. General Douglas MacArthur, representing the Allied powers, accepted the surrender on behalf of the United States. The signing of the surrender marked the official conclusion of World War II and a turning point in global history.

The news of Japan's surrender was met with jubilation and relief across the world. In the United States and other Allied countries, celebrations erupted in the streets. People rejoiced, waved flags, and hugged one another, expressing their gratitude that the war was finally over. V-J Day was a moment of shared victory and unity, demonstrating the strength of international cooperation and the resilience of humanity in the face of adversity.

The aftermath of V-J Day brought about a period of rebuilding and recovery. The war's impact was profound, and nations worked together to reconstruct their economies, infrastructure, and societies. The collective desire for lasting peace led to the establishment of international organizations like the United Nations, aimed at preventing future conflicts and fostering diplomacy.

V-J Day remains a poignant reminder of the sacrifices made during World War II and the importance of working together to overcome challenges. It serves as a testament to the human spirit's capacity to persevere, even in the darkest times. The celebrations that erupted on that day reflected a universal longing for peace, stability, and a better future for generations to come.

Nuremberg Trials

The Nuremberg Trials, held in the aftermath of World War II, were a series of military tribunals that sought to bring prominent leaders of the Third Reich to justice for their role in war crimes and crimes against humanity. The trials took place in the city of Nuremberg, Germany, between November 20, 1945, and October 1, 1946, marking a historic moment in the pursuit of international justice.

The primary objective of the Nuremberg Trials was to hold accountable those responsible for atrocities committed during the war. The major war criminals, including high-ranking military officials, politicians, and industrialists, were indicted and prosecuted for crimes such as genocide, crimes against peace, and war crimes. The trials represented a collective effort by the Allied powers, namely the United States, the Soviet Union, the United Kingdom, and France, to establish a legal framework for addressing the unprecedented crimes committed by the Nazi regime.

One of the key legal innovations of the Nuremberg Trials was the establishment of the principles that would guide subsequent international prosecutions. The trials introduced the concept of individual criminal responsibility, emphasizing that individuals could be held accountable for their actions, even if they were acting on behalf of a state. This marked a departure from traditional notions of state immunity.

The defendants faced charges that encompassed a range of offenses, from planning and waging aggressive war to committing atrocities against civilians and prisoners of war. The prosecution presented extensive evidence, including documents, photographs, and witness testimonies, to build its case against the accused. The trials were conducted before an International Military Tribunal (IMT) composed of judges from the four Allied powers.

Notable figures among the defendants included Hermann Göring, Rudolf Hess, Joachim von Ribbentrop, and Albert

Speer. The trials addressed not only the crimes committed by the military but also those perpetrated by the Nazi Party and its various organizations. The proceedings aimed to unveil the scope of the atrocities committed by the Nazi regime and hold accountable those who played significant roles in planning and executing these actions.

The Nuremberg Trials were not without controversy. Some critics argued that the trials represented a form of "victor's justice," as the Allied powers were both judges and prosecutors. However, the trials were viewed as an essential step in establishing the principles of international law and accountability for war crimes. They set important precedents for subsequent trials, including those held for crimes committed in the former Yugoslavia, Rwanda, and the International Criminal Court.

The verdicts were handed down on October 1, 1946. Twelve of the defendants were sentenced to death, three were acquitted, and others received various prison terms. The sentences were carried out on October 16, 1946, marking the first time in history that high-ranking political and military leaders were executed for crimes against humanity.

The legacy of the Nuremberg Trials extends beyond the courtroom. They played a pivotal role in shaping modern international law and establishing the principle that individuals, regardless of their official positions, could be held accountable for egregious violations of human rights. The trials aimed to bring justice to the victims of the Holocaust and other wartime atrocities while sending a powerful message about the consequences of engaging in aggressive warfare and committing crimes against humanity. The Nuremberg Trials stand as a landmark moment in the quest for justice and the prevention of future atrocities on the global stage.

Recovery and the Marshall Plan

World War II brought about widespread destruction and devastation across Europe, leaving nations grappling with the daunting task of rebuilding their societies, economies, and infrastructure. The aftermath of the war presented a unique challenge as countries sought to recover from the ravages of conflict and establish a foundation for lasting peace. Central to this effort was the Marshall Plan, a comprehensive aid program that played a pivotal role in the recovery and reconstruction of war-torn Europe.

As the war ended in 1945, Europe faced an overwhelming array of challenges. Cities lay in ruins, industries were in shambles, and millions of people were displaced from their homes. The economic fabric of many nations had been torn apart, and there was a pressing need to revive economies, provide essential resources, and restore stability. The Marshall Plan, officially known as the European Recovery Program, emerged as a bold and visionary initiative to address these urgent needs.

The Marshall Plan, named after U.S. Secretary of State George C. Marshall, aimed to bolster Europe's recovery by providing substantial financial assistance. Announced in 1947, the plan offered direct economic aid to European nations devastated by the war. The United States committed to supplying billions of dollars in financial aid, technical expertise, and resources to aid reconstruction efforts. The plan was open to all European countries, including those in the Eastern Bloc, but was most readily accepted by Western European nations.

The goals of the Marshall Plan were multifold. First, it sought to provide immediate relief to nations struggling with food shortages, housing crises, and other basic needs. By delivering food, fuel, and essential commodities, the plan aimed to stabilize the dire situations in these countries. Second, it aimed to stimulate economic recovery by injecting capital into industries and businesses. This not only spurred economic growth but also created jobs, jump-starting the process of rebuilding. Third, the plan fostered cooperation and collaboration among European nations, aiming to create stronger diplomatic ties and reduce the potential for future conflicts.

The Marshall Plan's implementation was met with a mix of enthusiasm and skepticism among European nations. While some countries readily embraced the aid, others were concerned about potential strings attached to American assistance. Nevertheless, over the course of the program's four years, from 1948 to 1952, over $13 billion in aid was distributed, positively impacting the economic recovery of numerous nations.

The impact of the Marshall Plan was profound and far-reaching. By 1952, industrial production in Western Europe had surpassed pre-war levels, signaling a remarkable turnaround. Infrastructure was rebuilt, trade networks were revitalized, and living standards began to rise. The plan played a vital role in reducing the specter of hunger, poverty, and instability that had haunted Europe in the immediate aftermath of the war.

Moreover, the Marshall Plan had significant geopolitical implications. It helped counteract the spread of communism in Western Europe by providing a viable alternative to the allure of the Eastern Bloc. By fostering economic prosperity, the plan laid the foundation for political stability and democratic governance in many nations.

Aircraft Carriers

Aircraft carriers played a pivotal role in World War II, revolutionizing naval warfare and becoming instrumental in shaping the outcome of the conflict. These massive ships were floating airbases, equipped with flight decks to launch and recover aircraft, making them a crucial asset in projecting power across vast ocean expanses.

At the outset of the war, aircraft carriers were relatively new, but their significance was quickly recognized by both the Allies and the Axis powers. The United States, Japan, and Great Britain were at the forefront of carrier development, while other nations also utilized carriers to varying degrees.

The aircraft carrier's most significant advantage was its ability to extend the reach of airpower far beyond traditional naval boundaries. Carriers enabled the deployment of fighter planes, dive bombers, and torpedo bombers, providing air support and engaging enemy ships, submarines, and aircraft. This versatility allowed carriers to adapt to various combat scenarios and provide critical support during major naval battles.

One of the most notable engagements involving aircraft carriers was the Battle of Midway in June 1942. The United States Navy's carriers, led by Admiral Chester W. Nimitz, successfully ambushed and devastated the Japanese carrier fleet. The decisive victory shifted the balance of power in the Pacific theater and marked a turning point in the war.

The Japanese also demonstrated the power of carriers during their surprise attack on Pearl Harbor in December 1941. In a daring move, carrier-based aircraft launched a surprise assault on the U.S. Pacific Fleet, causing significant damage and drawing the United States into the war.

Aircraft carriers were not only crucial in naval battles but also played a vital role in supporting amphibious landings. During major operations like D-Day in Normandy, carriers provided air cover for troops landing on the beaches, neutralizing enemy defenses and ensuring a safer approach for ground forces.

Throughout the war, carriers participated in numerous major engagements, such as the Battle of the Coral Sea, the Battle of Leyte Gulf, and the Battle of the Philippine Sea. These battles often featured carrier-based aircraft engaging in intense dogfights and carrying out devastating bombing runs on enemy ships.

While carriers brought immense advantages, they also faced significant risks. The Battle of the Eastern Solomons in August 1942 and the Battle of Santa Cruz Islands in October 1942 saw both American and Japanese carriers sustaining heavy damage or sinking. The vulnerability of carriers highlighted the importance of effective air cover and anti-aircraft defenses.

By the war's end, aircraft carriers had firmly established themselves as indispensable naval assets. Their strategic flexibility, ability to project airpower over long distances, and capability to support ground operations made them the backbone of modern naval warfare. The lessons learned from World War II influenced the continued development and expansion of aircraft carrier fleets in the post-war era.

Role of Aircraft in World War II

World War II marked a pivotal era in the history of aviation, with aircraft playing a vital role in shaping the outcome of the conflict. From the skies over Europe to the vast Pacific Ocean, the performance and capabilities of warplanes had a profound impact on the battles and strategies of the war. These flying machines evolved rapidly during the war, becoming faster, more agile, and more lethal, ultimately becoming a decisive factor in the triumph of the Allied forces.

During World War II, aircraft were used for various critical missions, including reconnaissance, bombing, dogfighting, and troop transport. Early in the war, reconnaissance planes provided valuable intelligence, allowing commanders to understand enemy positions and movements. This information was crucial in planning military strategies and coordinating ground forces effectively.

One of the most iconic roles of aircraft in World War II was their use in bombing campaigns. Both Axis and Allied forces employed bombers to attack enemy targets on land and at sea. The bombing raids devastated cities, infrastructure, and industrial centers, disrupting the enemy's production capabilities and weakening their resolve. Notably, strategic bombing played a significant role in the eventual Allied victory in Europe.

Air superiority was a key factor in determining the outcome of battles, and dogfighting, or aerial combat, became a critical component of air warfare. Fighter planes engaged in intense aerial duels to gain control of the skies and protect friendly forces from enemy attacks. The most famous fighter planes of the war included the British Spitfire, the American P-51 Mustang, and the German Messerschmitt Bf 109. These nimble and deadly aircraft were piloted by skilled airmen who exhibited remarkable courage and skill.

Transport aircraft also played a vital role in the war effort, enabling the rapid movement of troops, supplies, and equipment. These planes were instrumental in conducting airborne operations, such as the famous D-Day invasion of Normandy in 1944. They allowed for the swift deployment of troops behind enemy lines, supporting major offensives and strategic maneuvers.

Technological advancements in aviation during World War II were significant. Jet engines were introduced, offering higher speeds and greater maneuverability, revolutionizing air combat. The German Messerschmitt Me 262 was the world's first operational jet-powered fighter aircraft, which showcased the potential of this new technology. The development of radar systems also played a critical role in providing early warning of approaching enemy aircraft and improving the accuracy of bombing runs.

Notably, the role of aircraft was not limited to the battlefield. In the Pacific Theater, aircraft carriers became floating airbases, allowing aircraft to project power across vast ocean expanses. The aircraft carrier battles of Midway and Coral Sea were pivotal engagements that demonstrated the importance of naval aviation in the Pacific campaign.

By the end of World War II, the skies were dominated by technologically advanced aircraft, and air power had become an integral component of military strategy. The flexibility and versatility of these warplanes provided a decisive advantage to the Allied forces. From the daring Doolittle Raid to the dogfights of the Battle of Britain, aircraft proved to be the wings of victory in a global conflict that reshaped the world's geopolitical landscape.

B-17 Flying Fortress

The B-17 Flying Fortress was a renowned heavy bomber used by the United States Army Air Forces (USAAF) during World War II. Developed and manufactured by Boeing, the B-17 played a significant role in the Allied air campaign, particularly in the European Theater of Operations. Its name, "Flying Fortress," stemmed from its impressive defensive armament and ability to withstand enemy attacks.

The B-17 had a remarkable range, allowing it to undertake long-range strategic bombing missions. It was capable of flying distances of up to 2,000 miles without refueling, making it a formidable force in reaching targets deep within enemy territory. This capability allowed the B-17 to participate in critical bombing campaigns against German industrial centers and military installations.

Crewed by ten men, the B-17 Flying Fortress was a formidable flying machine. The crew included a pilot, co-pilot, bombardier, navigator, radio operator, flight engineer, and four gunners manning its numerous defensive positions. The aircraft's size and crew complement made it one of the largest bombers of its time.

One of the most notable features of the B-17 was its formidable defensive armament. It was equipped with up to thirteen .50 caliber machine guns, providing extensive coverage against enemy fighter attacks. These guns were mounted in multiple turrets, including the top, bottom, front, rear, and sides of the aircraft. The firepower of the B-17 made it a challenging target for enemy fighters, and it earned a reputation for its ability to fend off attacks.

The B-17 Flying Fortress played a crucial role in the strategic bombing campaign against Nazi Germany during World War II. Its ability to carry a significant bomb load and its long-range capabilities made it a formidable weapon against German industrial and military targets. It participated in key missions, such as the daylight bombing campaign against German aircraft factories and ball-bearing plants.

Beyond its strategic bombing role, the B-17 also conducted missions to support ground forces during the war. It provided close air support, dropping bombs on enemy positions and supply lines to assist allied troops in their advances.

The B-17 Flying Fortress, with its iconic design and formidable capabilities, symbolized the United States' commitment to aerial warfare during World War II. Its effectiveness in combat and the dedication of its crew made it an essential component of the Allied war effort. The B-17's contribution to the air campaign in Europe played a significant role in weakening German war production and ultimately contributed to the defeat of Nazi Germany.

The legacy of the B-17 Flying Fortress extends beyond its wartime service. Many B-17s have been preserved and restored, serving as flying museums and historical reminders of the courage and sacrifice of the crews who flew them during World War II. Today, the B-17 remains an enduring symbol of American air power and the brave men who flew these mighty Flying Fortresses into the heat of battle.

Enola Gay

The Enola Gay is a historically significant aircraft from World War II, known for its pivotal role in a momentous event. This B-29 Superfortress bomber played a crucial part in shaping the outcome of the war and leaving a lasting impact on history.

The Enola Gay was a B-29 aircraft, a type of heavy bomber, used by the United States during World War II. It was a special plane, distinguishable by its silver finish and the iconic name painted on its nose. The Enola Gay carried an important mission, and its crew became instrumental in the events that followed.

The crew of the Enola Gay consisted of twelve members. The pilot was Colonel Paul W. Tibbets Jr., who named the aircraft after his mother, Enola Gay Tibbets. The aircraft's name was a tribute to his mother's support and love. The crew also included bombardier Major Thomas Ferebee and navigator Theodore "Dutch" Van Kirk, among others. These individuals would be forever associated with the Enola Gay and its historic mission.

The Enola Gay's most famous engagement was the bombing of Hiroshima on August 6, 1945. This mission marked a turning point in World War II, as it led to the surrender of Japan and the end of the war. The Enola Gay carried the "Little Boy" atomic bomb, which was dropped over Hiroshima, causing immense destruction and loss of life. This event marked the first use of a nuclear weapon in warfare and had profound implications for the world.

The Enola Gay's significance in World War II cannot be overstated. The bombing of Hiroshima not only hastened the end of the war but also ushered in the nuclear age and reshaped global politics and warfare. The immense power of the atomic bomb demonstrated by the Enola Gay changed the way nations approached conflict and diplomacy.

Today, the Enola Gay is preserved and displayed at the National Air and Space Museum's Steven F. Udvar-Hazy Center in Chantilly, Virginia, USA. The aircraft underwent extensive restoration to ensure its preservation and to present an accurate historical record. Visitors can see the Enola Gay up close, learning about its history and the significant role it played in World War II.

The Luftwaffe

The Luftwaffe, or the German Air Force, played a pivotal role in shaping the course of World War II and military aviation history. Established in 1935 as part of the rearmament efforts of Nazi Germany under the leadership of Adolf Hitler, the Luftwaffe quickly rose to become one of the most formidable air forces in the world. With its innovative tactics, advanced aircraft designs, and skilled pilots, the Luftwaffe posed a significant threat to its adversaries and exerted a profound influence on the outcome of the war.

At the onset of World War II in 1939, the Luftwaffe unleashed a devastating aerial campaign known as the Blitzkrieg, or "lightning war," which relied on rapid and coordinated air attacks to overwhelm enemy defenses. This strategy was demonstrated with chilling effectiveness during the invasion of Poland, where Luftwaffe bombers conducted relentless bombing raids, targeting military installations, infrastructure, and civilian centers. The Blitzkrieg tactics were further refined and employed with devastating effect in subsequent campaigns, including the invasions of France, the Low Countries, and the Soviet Union.

One of the Luftwaffe's most iconic aircraft during the early years of the war was the Messerschmitt Bf 109, a versatile and highly maneuverable fighter plane that dominated the skies over Europe. Supported by formidable bombers such as the Junkers Ju 87 Stuka and the Heinkel He 111, the Luftwaffe achieved air superiority over much of the continent, allowing German ground forces to advance rapidly and secure key objectives.

However, the Luftwaffe faced significant challenges as the war progressed, particularly in the face of determined Allied resistance and technological advancements. The introduction of more capable Allied fighter aircraft, such as the British Spitfire and the American P-51 Mustang, posed a formidable threat to Luftwaffe dominance in the air. Additionally, the strategic bombing campaign waged by the Allies, particularly the British Royal Air Force's night raids and the United States Army Air Forces' daylight bombings, inflicted heavy losses on Luftwaffe aircraft and infrastructure, crippling its ability to sustain offensive operations.

The turning point for the Luftwaffe came with the Battle of Britain in 1940, a pivotal aerial campaign that saw the Luftwaffe engage in a protracted air battle with the Royal Air Force over the skies of southern England. Despite initially achieving tactical victories and inflicting heavy losses on British airfields and cities, the Luftwaffe ultimately failed to gain air superiority, thwarting Hitler's plans for a seaborne invasion of Britain and marking the first major setback for the German war machine.

The Luftwaffe's fortunes continued to decline as the war progressed, with its aircraft and pilots stretched thin on multiple fronts. The costly aerial battles on the Eastern Front against the Soviet Union and the relentless bombing raids over Germany by Allied air forces exacted a heavy toll on Luftwaffe personnel and resources. By the war's end in 1945, the Luftwaffe had been severely weakened, its once-mighty air force reduced to a shadow of its former self.

Despite its eventual defeat, the Luftwaffe remains a symbol of innovation, skill, and determination in the annals of military aviation history. Its pioneering tactics, technological advancements, and contributions to the development of aerial warfare have left an indelible mark on the modern concept of air power. Today, the legacy of the Luftwaffe serves as a reminder of the complex and dynamic nature of air warfare and the enduring impact of World War II on the evolution of military strategy and technology.

The British Spitfire

The Supermarine Spitfire, an iconic British fighter aircraft, played a pivotal role in World War II and stands as a symbol of British resilience and technological prowess. Designed by R.J. Mitchell, the Spitfire was a key component of the Royal Air Force's (RAF) air defense during the war, renowned for its agility, speed, and adaptability.

The Spitfire's development began in the mid-1930s as tensions escalated in Europe. Its maiden flight took place in March 1936, and by the time World War II erupted in 1939, the Spitfire was already in service. The aircraft's distinctive elliptical wing design, a hallmark of Mitchell's innovation, contributed to its exceptional maneuverability and overall performance.

Powered by various engines throughout its production, including the Rolls-Royce Merlin and Griffon, the Spitfire could achieve speeds of over 360 miles per hour, making it one of the fastest fighters of its time. Its Rolls-Royce Merlin engine, in particular, played a crucial role in its success, providing the aircraft with the power needed for high-speed interception and combat.

The Spitfire became synonymous with the Battle of Britain, a critical aerial campaign fought over the skies of England in 1940. Facing off against the German Luftwaffe, the Spitfire, along with the Hawker Hurricane, successfully defended British airspace, preventing a German invasion. The aircraft's agility and firepower, often armed with eight .303 Browning machine guns, contributed to its success in dogfights against enemy aircraft.

Beyond its role in air defense, the Spitfire adapted to various roles throughout the war. It served as a fighter-bomber, reconnaissance aircraft, and escort for bomber formations. The Spitfire's versatility and continuous upgrades allowed it to remain relevant in changing combat scenarios.

One of the most famous versions of the Spitfire was the Spitfire Mk IX, introduced in 1942. This model featured an improved Merlin engine and addressed some of the earlier versions' limitations at higher altitudes. The Mk IX became a formidable adversary for German aircraft and played a crucial role in maintaining air superiority over Western Europe.

The Spitfire's impact extended beyond its military capabilities; it became a symbol of British defiance and determination. Its distinctive silhouette and the "Spitfire Spirit" embodied the resilience of the RAF and the British people during a challenging period in history.

Post-war, the Spitfire continued to serve in various air forces around the world, including in conflicts such as the Arab-Israeli War of 1948. Its legacy endured not only in military aviation but also in popular culture, with the Spitfire featuring prominently in films, documentaries, and airshows.

Several Spitfires have been preserved and restored, with enthusiasts and collectors maintaining these historic aircraft. The Battle of Britain Memorial Flight in the United Kingdom, for example, keeps Spitfires airworthy, allowing current generations to witness the aircraft in flight and appreciate its significance.

In conclusion, the Supermarine Spitfire stands as a testament to British engineering excellence and the bravery of the RAF during World War II. From its critical role in the Battle of Britain to its adaptability in various combat scenarios, the Spitfire earned its place as one of the most celebrated and recognizable aircraft in aviation history. Its enduring legacy continues to capture the imagination of aviation enthusiasts and serves as a reminder of the courage and skill displayed by those who flew this remarkable fighter during a pivotal period in the 20th century.

German ME-262 Fighter

The Messerschmitt Me 262, a revolutionary fighter jet developed by Nazi Germany during World War II, stands as a pioneering example of jet-powered aviation. As the world's first operational jet-powered fighter aircraft, the Me 262 played a significant role in shaping the future of aerial warfare.

Designed by German engineer Willy Messerschmitt, the Me 262 was conceived to counter Allied air superiority. Its development began in the early 1940s, and the first prototype took to the skies in April 1941. However, various challenges, including engine development issues, delayed its full-scale production until later in the war.

The Me 262's sleek and aerodynamic design contributed to its exceptional speed and performance. Powered by twin Junkers Jumo 004 engines, the Me 262 could reach speeds of up to 840 kilometers per hour (about 522 miles per hour), far surpassing the capabilities of traditional propeller-driven aircraft of the time. This speed advantage allowed the Me 262 to engage and evade enemy fighters more effectively.

Armed with a nose-mounted MK 108 30mm cannon and a quartet of MK 108 or MG 151/20 20mm cannons, the Me 262 posed a formidable threat to Allied bombers and fighter planes. Its firepower and speed made it a challenging adversary, as it could quickly close in on its targets, inflict damage, and escape before opponents could react.

The Me 262 made its combat debut in July 1944, marking a new era in aviation warfare. Its appearance startled Allied pilots, who were accustomed to slower propeller-driven aircraft. The Me 262's ability to intercept and engage enemy planes with relative ease initially caught the Allies off guard.

Despite its technological advancements, the Me 262 faced challenges, including limited production capacity and fuel shortages. The German war machine was strained, and the Me 262's impact on the outcome of the war was limited by factors beyond its technological superiority. Its introduction came at a time when Germany was already on the defensive, and the Allies' strategic bombing campaign had significantly weakened German industrial capabilities.

The Me 262's role in air combat was diverse, ranging from bomber interception to ground attack missions. It could carry a variety of ordnance, including bombs and unguided rockets, making it a versatile platform. However, its full potential was never realized due to the constraints imposed by Germany's wartime situation.

The Me 262 influenced post-war aviation developments significantly. Its success in jet-powered flight demonstrated the viability and superiority of jet engines over traditional propeller-driven designs. The technological advancements introduced by the Me 262 laid the groundwork for the development of subsequent generations of jet fighters.

In the post-war era, various nations sought to understand and replicate the technology behind the Me 262. The aircraft's impact resonated in the design of subsequent jet fighters, contributing to the evolution of aerial combat capabilities globally.

Today, the Messerschmitt Me 262 remains an iconic symbol of World War II aviation technology. Several examples have been preserved in museums around the world, allowing enthusiasts and historians to appreciate the groundbreaking engineering and design that went into creating the world's first operational jet-powered fighter aircraft. The Me 262's legacy endures as a testament to the rapid technological advancements that took place during a pivotal period in aviation history.

Japanese Zero

The Japanese Zero fighter plane, officially known as the Mitsubishi A6M Zero, stands as one of the most iconic aircraft of World War II, renowned for its agility, speed, and distinctive presence in the Pacific theater. Designed by Mitsubishi's Jiro Horikoshi, the Zero played a pivotal role in Japan's early wartime successes, showcasing its excellence in dogfighting and aerial maneuvers.

Armed with two 7.7mm machine guns and two 20mm cannon, the Zero was a formidable fighter with a streamlined design that allowed it to outmaneuver adversaries in close-quarters combat. Its lightweight construction and innovative engineering contributed to its remarkable agility, making it a masterful dogfighter.

The Zero's speed and maneuverability were key features that set it apart. With a top speed of around 330 miles per hour (531 kilometers per hour), it could compete with many of its contemporaries. Its extended range, thanks to large internal fuel tanks, allowed it to operate over considerable distances, giving it an edge in long-range missions and surprise attacks.

The Zero's combat engagements showcased its prowess in the Pacific theater. In the early stages of the war, during Japan's expansion, the Zero's advanced technology and exceptional performance often caught Allied forces off guard. The plane was most known for its participation in the attack on Pearl Harbor in December 1941, which marked Japan's entrance into World War II. The Zero's speed and maneuverability allowed it to dominate aerial battles during Japan's initial offensives.

Approximately 10,939 Zero fighter planes were built during the course of the war, with various models and modifications introduced to enhance performance. The plane's agility, combined with the skills of its pilots, often granted Japan a tactical advantage in dogfights, especially against larger and heavier American aircraft.

Despite its early successes, the Zero's significance in the Pacific theater gradually diminished as the war progressed. Advancements in Allied aircraft design and tactics eventually exposed some of the Zero's vulnerabilities, such as its lack of self-sealing fuel tanks and armor protection for the pilot. These weaknesses became evident in the face of more modern and powerful opponents.

By the mid-war years, the Zero's limitations led to a decline in its effectiveness, as newer Allied planes gained superiority in both firepower and armor. Pilots faced increasing challenges in combat, and the Zero's reputation as an unbeatable adversary began to wane.

In conclusion, the Japanese Zero fighter plane, known for its agility, speed, and early wartime successes, played a significant role in the Pacific theater during World War II. With its streamlined design, formidable armaments, and exceptional maneuverability, it was a symbol of Japanese air power in the early stages of the conflict. While its impact on the war waned as Allied technology and tactics evolved, the Zero's legacy endures as a symbol of Japan's early aerial dominance and its role in shaping the air battles of the Pacific.

P-51 Mustang

The P-51 Mustang was a legendary fighter aircraft that played a crucial role in World War II. Designed and produced by North American Aviation, the Mustang was an American long-range fighter and bomber escort, becoming one of the most effective and iconic aircraft of the war.

The development of the P-51 Mustang began in the early 1940s, in response to the British Royal Air Force's request for a high-performance fighter. The original model, powered by an Allison V-1710 engine, showed promise but lacked high-altitude performance. However, with the introduction of the British Rolls-Royce Merlin engine, the Mustang's capabilities were dramatically enhanced, and it became a formidable opponent.

The Mustang's speed, agility, and long-range capabilities made it an ideal escort for Allied bombers on strategic bombing missions deep into enemy territory. With the P-51's arrival, the Allied bombers finally had the necessary protection to overcome the formidable Luftwaffe, the German air force. The Mustang's range allowed it to accompany bombers all the way to Berlin and back, providing critical air support and safeguarding the bombers against enemy fighter attacks.

In addition to its escort role, the P-51 was also highly successful in aerial combat against enemy aircraft. Its impressive speed and maneuverability allowed it to engage and outperform the German Messerschmitt Bf 109 and the Focke-Wulf Fw 190. The Mustang's powerful armament, consisting of six .50 caliber machine guns, enabled it to effectively engage enemy fighters and bombers.

One of the most notable versions of the P-51 was the P-51D Mustang. This variant featured a "bubble" canopy that provided improved visibility for the pilot and additional fuel tanks that further extended its range. The P-51D became the most produced version of the aircraft and played a significant role in the later stages of the war.

The P-51 Mustang's impact on World War II was profound, as it played a critical role in achieving air superiority for the Allies. Its effectiveness in bomber escort missions allowed the Allies to cripple German war industries and weaken the Nazi war effort. Furthermore, the Mustang's successes in air-to-air combat bolstered the confidence of Allied pilots and further secured air supremacy.

Beyond its wartime achievements, the P-51 Mustang left a lasting legacy in aviation history. It is widely regarded as one of the greatest fighter aircraft ever built and became a symbol of American ingenuity and engineering prowess. Even after World War II, the Mustang continued to serve in various air forces around the world, further cementing its place as an iconic aircraft that forever shaped the course of aviation.

Battleship Bismarck

The Battleship Bismarck was a remarkable warship that played a significant role during World War II. Built by Nazi Germany, this massive vessel was a symbol of the nation's naval power. The Bismarck was one of the largest battleships of its time, crewed by a dedicated team and armed with formidable weaponry. Its brief but intense engagements left a lasting impact on naval history.

Constructed in Hamburg, Germany, the Battleship Bismarck was an engineering marvel. It measured about 823 feet in length and had a displacement of over 50,000 tons. This immense size made the Bismarck an imposing force on the seas, capable of withstanding enemy attacks and projecting Germany's naval prowess.

The ship's crew consisted of around 2,200 men who operated various systems and functions. These dedicated sailors were responsible for maintaining the ship's operations, ensuring its effectiveness during battles, and maintaining its weaponry. The crew's commitment and coordination were crucial to the ship's overall success.

Armed with a fearsome array of weaponry, the Bismarck was a force to be reckoned with. It boasted eight 15-inch main guns, which could fire powerful shells over long distances with devastating accuracy. Additionally, the ship was equipped with secondary armaments, anti-aircraft guns, and torpedo tubes, making it a versatile combatant capable of engaging multiple types of threats.

The most famous engagement involving the Battleship Bismarck was its encounter with the British Royal Navy in May 1941. The Bismarck, along with the cruiser Prinz Eugen, embarked on a mission to disrupt Allied shipping in the Atlantic. The British quickly responded, launching a relentless pursuit to neutralize the German threat.

In the Battle of Denmark Strait, the Bismarck and Prinz Eugen engaged the British battlecruiser HMS Hood and the battleship HMS Prince of Wales. In a devastating moment, the Bismarck's accurate fire struck the HMS Hood, causing a catastrophic explosion that sank the British ship. This event shocked the world and highlighted the Bismarck's formidable firepower.

The Bismarck's success, however, was short-lived. The British Royal Navy relentlessly pursued the German battleship. In a daring effort, the Royal Navy's aircraft launched a torpedo attack, damaging the Bismarck's rudder and making it difficult for the ship to maneuver effectively. Soon after, British warships closed in and engaged the Bismarck in a ferocious battle.

Facing overwhelming odds, the Bismarck's crew fought valiantly, but the ship's fate was sealed. With its systems heavily damaged and the British closing in, the Bismarck was scuttled by its own crew to prevent capture. The once-mighty battleship succumbed to the depths of the Atlantic Ocean on May 27, 1941.

The Battleship Bismarck's legacy remains a mix of awe and respect. Its size, armaments, and engagements demonstrated the capabilities of naval technology during World War II. The ship's resilience and the dedication of its crew stand as a testament to the fierce determination of those who served on it. Despite its short operational life, the Battleship Bismarck left an indelible mark on naval history and the memory of its dramatic battles lives on as a symbol of wartime naval prowess.

Battleship Yamato

The Battleship Yamato, a colossal warship of World War II, stands as a symbol of Japan's naval might and the era's fierce conflicts. This massive vessel, with a crew of over 2,700, played a significant role in maritime warfare due to its size, armament, and engagements.

With a length stretching over 860 feet, the Yamato was a behemoth on the seas. Its imposing size allowed it to carry an array of powerful armaments, including nine 18.1-inch main guns, the largest ever mounted on a battleship. Alongside these main guns were smaller cannons, antiaircraft guns, and torpedoes, creating a formidable arsenal capable of engaging threats from air, sea, and land.

The Yamato was not just a battleship; it was a symbol of Japan's determination and military strength. It played a crucial role in several pivotal battles, including the Battle of Leyte Gulf in 1944. However, its engagements often saw limited success due to the evolving tactics of naval warfare. The increasing dominance of aircraft carriers and airpower rendered large battleships vulnerable to aerial attacks.

The downfall of the Yamato came during Operation Ten-Go in 1945. Tasked with a last-ditch effort to counter Allied forces in Okinawa, the Yamato and its escorts faced relentless assaults from American aircraft and submarines. Despite valiant resistance, the Yamato succumbed to overwhelming firepower, eventually sinking beneath the waves. The loss of the Yamato marked the end of an era for battleships, as it highlighted the changing nature of naval warfare and the growing importance of aircraft carriers.

The significance of the Yamato extends beyond its military prowess. It represents the height of Japan's imperial ambitions during the war and the sacrifices made by its crew. The dedication of its sailors and the ship's imposing presence captured the imagination of people both in Japan and around the world. The Yamato's legacy endures as a reminder of the devastating impact of war and the complexities of military strategy.

In conclusion, the Battleship Yamato was a colossal warship that left an indelible mark on history. Its size, armament, engagements, and eventual downfall reflect the challenges faced by naval forces during World War II. Beyond its military significance, the Yamato remains a symbol of Japan's wartime aspirations and the sacrifices made by its crew. Its story serves as a reminder of the human cost of conflict and the evolving nature of warfare in the modern era.

U.S.S. Arizona

The U.S.S. Arizona stands as a powerful symbol of both American naval history and the tragic events of the Attack on Pearl Harbor. With a history that spans decades and a catastrophic fate that befell it on December 7, 1941, the ship remains a solemn reminder of the sacrifices made by those who served and the toll of war.

Commissioned in 1916 as a Pennsylvania-class battleship, the U.S.S. Arizona was a marvel of naval engineering. Spanning 608 feet in length and armed with twelve 14-inch guns, the ship was a formidable force on the seas. It played a significant role in the peacetime activities of the United States Navy, serving as a deterrent and a symbol of American maritime power during the interwar period.

However, the ship's history took a tragic turn on that fateful day in 1941. During the surprise Attack on Pearl Harbor launched by the Japanese Imperial Navy, the U.S.S. Arizona found itself under attack along with other American naval vessels. In a devastating blow, an armor-piercing bomb struck the forward magazine of the ship, triggering a massive explosion. The explosion ignited a fierce fire that rapidly consumed the ship, leading to its eventual sinking. The U.S.S. Arizona's stern remained above the waterline, serving as a haunting and painful reminder of the loss of life that occurred that day.

The toll of human lives lost on the U.S.S. Arizona was immense. Of the approximately 1,512 sailors and Marines on board during the attack, over 1,177 perished, many in the initial explosion or ensuing fires. The ship's rapid sinking created a dire situation, and the brave efforts of fellow sailors to rescue survivors and recover bodies amidst the chaos were met with immense challenges. The U.S.S. Arizona bore witness to the devastating consequences of war and the price of freedom.

The significance of the U.S.S. Arizona goes beyond its role as a casualty of war. It serves as a poignant reminder of the human cost of conflict and the sacrifices made by those who serve in the armed forces. In the aftermath of the attack, the wreckage of the ship remained submerged in the harbor, and efforts to salvage the ship were deemed too costly and complex. Instead, it was decided that the ship would serve as a memorial to honor the lives lost and the service of those who perished.

Today, the U.S.S. Arizona Memorial stands above the sunken remains of the ship, suspended above the water on a platform that allows visitors to pay their respects and reflect on the events of that tragic day. The memorial encompasses a wall of names that lists all the sailors and Marines who lost their lives on the ship. It is a place of solemnity and reverence, where visitors can learn about the history of the ship, the attack, and the individuals who served aboard.

Moreover, the U.S.S. Arizona Memorial is a unique and sacred place, as it serves as a final resting place for many of the sailors who lost their lives on the ship. The submerged hull of the ship is considered a cemetery, and several crew members who survived the attack later chose to be interred within the ship, laying with their shipmates for eternity.

In conclusion, the U.S.S. Arizona stands as a poignant reminder of the sacrifices made by those who served in the U.S. Navy during World War II. Its history, from its days as a battleship to its tragic sinking at Pearl Harbor, is a testament to the human cost of conflict. The U.S.S. Arizona Memorial serves as a place of remembrance, honoring the lives lost and preserving the memory of the ship's role in history.

U.S.S Iowa

The USS Iowa (BB-61), a renowned Iowa-class battleship, emerged as a formidable symbol of American naval power during World War II. Commissioned in 1943, the USS Iowa played a pivotal role in various Pacific Theater campaigns, showcasing its versatility and firepower. With its sleek design and advanced technology, the battleship earned a distinguished reputation that persisted throughout its operational history.

The USS Iowa was the lead ship of its class, characterized by its powerful main battery of nine 16-inch guns, impressive speed, and robust armor. Its primary armament, housed in three turrets, provided unparalleled firepower, making it a formidable force in naval engagements. The battleship's ability to deliver accurate and devastating fire contributed significantly to its effectiveness in various combat scenarios.

One of the USS Iowa's most notable contributions occurred during World War II in the Pacific. The battleship actively participated in significant campaigns, including the Battle of the Philippine Sea and the Battle of Leyte Gulf. Its presence in these engagements demonstrated the United States' commitment to projecting naval power in the vast expanses of the Pacific Ocean.

The Battle of Leyte Gulf, fought in October 1944, witnessed the USS Iowa as part of Admiral William Halsey's Third Fleet. During this engagement, the battleship played a crucial role in providing protective cover for aircraft carriers and engaging enemy surface vessels. The strategic importance of the battle, coupled with the USS Iowa's firepower, showcased the battleship's effectiveness in naval warfare.

The USS Iowa's versatility extended beyond its role in surface engagements. It served as the flagship for Admiral William Halsey during critical periods of the Pacific campaign. The battleship's advanced communication facilities and command capabilities made it an ideal platform for coordinating fleet movements and executing strategic decisions.

In addition to its involvement in the Pacific, the USS Iowa played a significant part in escorting President Franklin D. Roosevelt to the Tehran Conference in 1943. This historic event marked the first time a sitting U.S. president traveled overseas during wartime, highlighting the battleship's importance in diplomatic and strategic missions.

The end of World War II did not signal the retirement of the USS Iowa. Instead, the battleship remained an active participant in subsequent conflicts, including the Korean War. Its versatility was once again evident as it provided fire support for United Nations forces and conducted naval bombardments along the Korean coastline. The USS Iowa's adaptability to evolving military requirements underscored its enduring significance.

Decommissioned in 1958, the USS Iowa experienced periods of inactivity before being recommissioned in the 1980s under the Reagan administration. Refitted with modern technology and weaponry, the battleship returned to service, reaffirming its status as a symbol of American naval strength. It played a prominent role in the 1980s and 1990s, participating in training exercises and serving as a deterrent during the Cold War era.

The USS Iowa was finally decommissioned for the last time in 1990, marking the end of its active service. In recognition of its historical significance, the battleship has been preserved as a museum ship in San Pedro, California. Visitors can explore its decks, experience its history, and gain insights into the pivotal role it played in World War II and beyond.

In conclusion, the USS Iowa stands as a testament to American naval ingenuity and resilience during World War II. Its powerful armament, strategic importance in key battles, and adaptability in various roles solidified its place in naval history. As a museum ship, the USS Iowa continues to serve as a tangible reminder of the courage and determination displayed by the United States Navy during one of the most challenging periods in global history.

U.S.S New Jersey

The USS New Jersey (BB-62), an iconic Iowa-class battleship, left an indelible mark on World War II as a formidable symbol of American naval power. Commissioned on May 23, 1943, the USS New Jersey played a crucial role in pivotal Pacific Theater campaigns, earning a reputation for its versatility, firepower, and strategic significance.

As the lead ship of its class, the USS New Jersey boasted a powerful main battery of nine 16-inch guns, arranged in three turrets, showcasing its formidable firepower. Its sleek design, impressive speed, and robust armor contributed to its effectiveness in naval engagements. The battleship's primary armament allowed it to deliver accurate and devastating fire, making it a potent force in various combat scenarios.

During World War II, the USS New Jersey actively participated in critical Pacific campaigns, including the Battle of the Philippine Sea and the Battle of Leyte Gulf. In these engagements, the battleship showcased its versatility and played a pivotal role in the United States' efforts to establish naval dominance in the vast expanses of the Pacific Ocean.

The Battle of Leyte Gulf, fought in October 1944, saw the USS New Jersey as part of Admiral William Halsey's Third Fleet. The battleship provided protective cover for aircraft carriers and engaged enemy surface vessels, contributing significantly to the success of the strategic battle. Its firepower and strategic importance underscored the battleship's effectiveness in naval warfare.

Beyond its role in surface engagements, the USS New Jersey served as the flagship for Admiral William Halsey during crucial periods of the Pacific campaign. Its advanced communication facilities and command capabilities made it an ideal platform for coordinating fleet movements and executing strategic decisions. The battleship's adaptability extended beyond combat, playing a key role in diplomatic and strategic missions.

In 1943, the USS New Jersey played a notable part in escorting President Franklin D. Roosevelt to the Tehran Conference. This historic event marked the first time a sitting U.S. president traveled overseas during wartime, highlighting the battleship's importance in both military and diplomatic spheres.

The end of World War II did not signal the retirement of the USS New Jersey. The battleship continued its service in subsequent conflicts, including the Korean War. During this period, it provided fire support for United Nations forces and conducted naval bombardments along the Korean coastline. The USS New Jersey's adaptability to evolving military requirements reaffirmed its enduring significance.

Decommissioned in 1948, the USS New Jersey experienced periods of inactivity before being recommissioned in the 1950s during the Korean War. Its advanced technology and weaponry were upgraded to meet modern standards, allowing it to continue its service. The battleship underwent further recommissioning in subsequent decades, including during the Vietnam War and the Cold War, showcasing its lasting impact on American naval power.

In 1991, the USS New Jersey was decommissioned for the last time. As a testament to its historical significance, the battleship has been preserved as a museum ship on the Camden Waterfront in New Jersey. Visitors can explore its decks, witness its history, and gain insights into the pivotal role it played in World War II and beyond. The USS New Jersey stands as a tangible reminder of the courage and determination displayed by the United States Navy during one of the most challenging periods in global history.

German Submarine Wolfpack

In the treacherous waters of World War II, German submarine wolfpacks emerged as a formidable and deadly threat to Allied convoys and merchant ships. These wolfpacks, also known as U-boat packs, were a strategic naval tactic employed by the German Kriegsmarine to disrupt vital supply lines and inflict heavy losses on Allied forces. Their devastating impact on maritime operations played a significant role in the early years of the war, earning them a fearsome reputation on the high seas.

The German Submarine Wolfpack strategy was based on a simple but effective principle: U-boats, or submarines, would group together and attack Allied shipping in concentrated assaults. This tactic aimed to overwhelm the convoy's defenses, making it easier for U-boats to sink multiple vessels in a single coordinated attack. The wolfpacks were particularly lethal during the Battle of the Atlantic, a long and grueling campaign that aimed to cut off the lifeline of supplies flowing from North America to Britain.

To execute a wolfpack attack, U-boats relied on radio communications to coordinate their positions and synchronize their assaults. A central command, usually a U-boat carrying a senior officer known as the "wolfpack commander," would direct the actions of the other submarines, guiding them toward the targeted convoy.

The wolfpacks struck with stealth and precision, often using the cover of darkness and adverse weather conditions to their advantage. Once the U-boats spotted their prey, they launched torpedoes from a distance, aiming to cripple the convoy's defense and cargo-carrying vessels. Following the initial attack, the U-boats would submerge and evade counterattacks from Allied escorts, which included warships and aircraft.

The German Submarine Wolfpacks enjoyed great success during the early years of World War II. Their relentless assaults led to heavy losses of Allied shipping and caused widespread disruption to the flow of supplies. At their peak, the wolfpacks inflicted a severe toll on the Allied war effort, nearly pushing Britain to the brink of defeat due to shortages of essential goods and fuel.

However, the Allies were not willing to succumb to the U-boat menace. With advancements in technology and improvements in anti-submarine warfare tactics, they gradually gained the upper hand. The introduction of long-range aircraft patrols, sonar detection systems, and the development of the convoy system, where merchant ships were protected by military escorts, began to turn the tide.

As the war progressed, the wolfpack strategy faced increasing challenges. The loss of experienced U-boat crews, coupled with the Allies' growing ability to decode German radio communications, weakened the effectiveness of the wolfpack attacks. By mid-1943, the once formidable wolfpacks had lost much of their potency, and the initiative shifted in favor of the Allied forces.

Despite their eventual decline, the legacy of the German Submarine Wolfpacks left an enduring impact on naval warfare. The deadly efficiency of the U-boats forced the Allies to adapt their strategies and invest heavily in anti-submarine measures, leading to significant advancements in naval technology and tactics.

The Sherman Tank

The Sherman tank, officially designated as the M4 Medium Tank, was one of the most iconic and widely used armored vehicles of World War II. Manufactured primarily by the United States, the tank served as a stalwart ally for the Allied forces, playing a pivotal role in numerous battles and campaigns throughout the war.

The M4 Sherman was named after the American Civil War General William T. Sherman and was designed as a successor to the M3 Lee/Grant tanks. It first entered combat in 1942 and quickly became the backbone of the U.S. and Allied armored forces. The Sherman was characterized by its well-rounded performance, striking a balance between mobility, firepower, and protection.

During World War II, vast numbers of Sherman tanks were deployed by the Allied forces. Over 50,000 units were produced, making it one of the most prolific tanks of the war. Its availability and versatility made it a crucial asset in multiple theaters of operation, including the European, North African, and Pacific theaters.

The tank's crew typically consisted of five members: a commander, a driver, a co-driver/bow gunner, a loader, and a gunner. The commander played a vital role in coordinating the tank's actions, while the driver maneuvered the vehicle on the battlefield. The co-driver was responsible for operating the bow-mounted machine gun, and the loader and gunner worked in tandem to handle the tank's primary armament.

The Sherman was armed with a 75mm main gun in the early versions, which proved effective against most German tanks early in the war. Later variants were equipped with a more powerful 76mm main gun, providing improved armor-penetrating capabilities. The tank's secondary armament included one or more .30-caliber and .50-caliber machine guns, adding to its firepower and versatility in dealing with infantry threats.

Throughout World War II, the Sherman tank played a vital role in various significant conflicts. In the European theater, Shermans saw action during the North African Campaign, the invasion of Italy, and the D-Day landings in Normandy. The tank's ability to maneuver and provide effective support to infantry was critical in achieving success in these campaigns.

One of the most significant challenges the Sherman faced was its vulnerability to German heavy tanks, such as the Tiger and Panther. The Sherman's armor was not as thick as that of its German counterparts, making it susceptible to penetration from enemy fire. However, the Sherman's superior numbers, ease of production, and adaptability allowed it to remain a valuable asset on the battlefield.

The Sherman tank's role was not limited to the European theater alone. In the Pacific, Shermans were utilized in island-hopping campaigns, including battles on Guadalcanal, Tarawa, and Iwo Jima. They provided essential fire support and proved instrumental in the Allied victory in the Pacific theater.

Despite its limitations, the Sherman tank's widespread use and reliability made it an essential part of the Allied war effort in World War II. Its contribution to the war effort extended beyond direct combat, as it also played a crucial role in logistic support and engineering tasks. The Sherman's legacy endures as a symbol of Allied determination and ingenuity, representing the tenacity of the men who manned these armored giants on the battlefields of World War II.

The Tiger Tank

The Tiger tank, officially designated as the Panzerkampfwagen VI Tiger, was one of the most fearsome and powerful armored vehicles deployed by the German Wehrmacht during World War II. Renowned for its imposing size, thick armor, and devastating firepower, the Tiger played a significant role in various critical conflicts throughout the war.

Designed in response to the Soviet T-34 and KV-1 tanks, the Tiger first entered combat in 1942. Its primary objective was to counter the increasing dominance of heavily armored enemy tanks on the Eastern Front. Manufactured in relatively small numbers due to its complexity and resource-intensive production, the Tiger was intended for specialized roles and strategic impact.

The Tiger tank's hallmark was its robust armor, particularly in the frontal sections. The hull and turret were reinforced with thick, sloped armor plates, providing unparalleled protection against most Allied tanks' standard armor-piercing rounds. Its 88mm KwK 36 main gun, originally an anti-aircraft gun, was repurposed for use in tank combat, becoming one of the most formidable tank guns of the war. The 88mm gun could penetrate most enemy armor at considerable ranges, outmatching the armaments of many Allied tanks.

The Tiger tank's crew typically consisted of five members: a commander, a gunner, a loader, a radio operator, and a driver. The commander played a critical role in directing the tank's actions on the battlefield, while the gunner and loader worked together to engage and reload the main gun efficiently. The radio operator was responsible for communications, and the driver maneuvered the tank during combat.

During World War II, the Tiger tank saw action in several significant conflicts. In the Eastern Front, Tigers were employed in critical battles such as the Battle of Kursk, where they faced Soviet tanks and anti-tank defenses. Despite their formidable capabilities, Tigers encountered challenges, such as mechanical breakdowns, fuel consumption, and transportation difficulties on poorly maintained roads and harsh terrain.

In North Africa, the Tiger tank was deployed during the North African Campaign, where it demonstrated its devastating firepower against Allied forces. Tiger tanks proved instrumental in gaining battlefield superiority during the initial phases of the campaign.

The Tiger's role extended to the Western Front as well, where it played a critical part in the Battle of Normandy following the D-Day landings. Despite the deployment of more advanced Allied tanks and improved anti-tank weaponry, the Tiger continued to pose a significant threat to the Allied forces.

The Tiger tank's limited production numbers and high resource demands prevented it from being a decisive factor in the war's outcome. However, its psychological impact on Allied troops was significant. The mere presence of a Tiger tank on the battlefield could instill fear and intimidation in enemy soldiers.

Ultimately, the Tiger's effectiveness was contingent on skilled crews and logistical support. While its thick armor and powerful gun gave it an advantage in head-to-head engagements, its mechanical reliability and logistical challenges sometimes hindered its performance.

The Tiger tank remains an iconic symbol of German armored might during World War II. Despite its limited deployment, it left a lasting impact on the evolution of armored warfare, prompting the development of new Allied tanks and anti-tank strategies.

A22 Churchill Tank

During World War II, the British A22 Churchill tank emerged as a distinctive and resilient armored vehicle, playing a vital role on various fronts. Renowned for its distinctive appearance and robust design, the Churchill earned a reputation for its durability and adaptability in the face of evolving battlefield challenges.

The Churchill tank was named after Prime Minister Winston Churchill and was designed to address the shortcomings of its predecessor, the Matilda. One of its defining features was its boxy, heavily armored hull, providing increased protection against enemy fire. The tank's frontal armor, in particular, was formidable, and this attribute earned the Churchill the nickname "Churchill's Fortress."

Equipped with a range of armaments, the Churchill tank had significant firepower. Its main armament varied across different marks, with options including the 2-pounder, 6-pounder, and 75mm guns. The versatility in armament allowed the Churchill to engage a variety of targets, from enemy tanks to fortified positions, making it a valuable asset in diverse combat scenarios.

Mobility, however, was initially a challenge for the Churchill. The early models were underpowered, and their speed was notably slow. Despite this limitation, the tank's durability and heavily armored design compensated for its lack of speed. Over time, improvements were made, and later models featured more powerful engines, enhancing the Churchill's overall mobility.

One of the Churchill's distinctive features was its ability to traverse challenging terrain. The tank's tracks and suspension system were well-suited for rough landscapes, providing it with the capability to navigate obstacles and difficult conditions. This feature allowed the Churchill to be effective in various theaters of war, from the Western Front in Europe to the deserts of North Africa.

The Churchill tank saw action in notable battles, including the Normandy landings in 1944. Its role extended beyond traditional tank duties; the Churchill was adapted for specialized tasks. Different variants were developed for purposes such as engineering, recovery, and flame-throwing. The Churchill AVRE (Armoured Vehicle Royal Engineers) was particularly noteworthy, featuring a specialized arm that could launch a petard mortar to breach obstacles and fortified positions.

Despite its resilience and adaptability, the Churchill did face challenges. Its slow speed made it susceptible to faster enemy tanks, especially in the later stages of the war when German armor improved. Additionally, the tank's silhouette and distinctive appearance made it an easy target for enemy artillery and aircraft.

The Churchill's contribution to the war effort extended beyond its combat capabilities. Its production and deployment played a significant role in maintaining British armored forces during critical phases of the conflict. The tank was well-regarded for its ability to absorb damage and protect its crew, instilling confidence among the soldiers who operated it.

In conclusion, the British A22 Churchill tank stands as a testament to adaptability and durability during World War II. Its distinctive design, combined with significant firepower and the ability to traverse challenging terrain, made it a valuable asset for the Allied forces. Despite its initial limitations, the Churchill played a vital role in various theaters of war, leaving an enduring mark on military history.

Type 97 Chi-Ha Tank

The Type 97 Chi-Ha tank was a prominent armored vehicle utilized by the Imperial Japanese Army during World War II. Introduced in the late 1930s, the Chi-Ha played a crucial role in various Pacific and Southeast Asian campaigns, showcasing its unique features and contributing to Japan's armored warfare capabilities.

One of the distinguishing characteristics of the Type 97 Chi-Ha was its moderate size and weight. Weighing around 15 tons, the tank featured a compact design that facilitated maneuverability in different terrains. Its dimensions, coupled with a relatively low profile, made it suitable for navigating through the dense jungles and challenging landscapes encountered in the Pacific theater.

The Chi-Ha was armed with a Type 97 57mm tank gun, which, while effective against infantry and lighter armored vehicles, proved somewhat inadequate against more heavily armored adversaries encountered in later stages of the war. Despite this limitation, the tank's firepower was respectable for its time, allowing it to engage a variety of targets on the battlefield.

One notable aspect of the Type 97 Chi-Ha was its riveted hull construction. Unlike some contemporary tanks that featured welded hulls, the Chi-Ha utilized riveting, which contributed to its distinctive appearance. The tank's armor, however, was relatively thin compared to some of its counterparts, making it vulnerable to more advanced anti-tank weaponry as the war progressed.

In terms of mobility, the Type 97 Chi-Ha demonstrated decent performance. Powered by a Mitsubishi Type 97 V-12 diesel engine, the tank had a top speed of approximately 38 km/h (24 mph). This allowed it to keep pace with infantry units during offensives and contribute to coordinated assaults.

The Chi-Ha tank saw extensive action in the early stages of World War II, contributing to Japan's successes in campaigns such as the invasion of Malaya and the Philippines. However, as the conflict progressed and the Allies developed more advanced tanks, the Type 97 faced challenges on the battlefield. Its limited armor and firepower became apparent, especially in encounters with heavily armored adversaries.

To address some of these shortcomings, the Japanese military introduced upgraded variants of the Chi-Ha, such as the Type 97 Shinhoto Chi-Ha, featuring a more potent 47mm tank gun. Despite these improvements, the Chi-Ha continued to face challenges against the technologically superior tanks fielded by the Allies.

The adaptability of the Type 97 Chi-Ha was evident in its various roles on the battlefield. Beyond its primary function as a battle tank, the Chi-Ha chassis served as the basis for specialized variants, including command tanks, flamethrower tanks, and self-propelled guns. These adaptations showcased the versatility of the Chi-Ha design, allowing it to fulfill different combat roles based on the evolving needs of the Japanese military.

In conclusion, the Type 97 Chi-Ha tank was a significant part of the Imperial Japanese Army's armored forces during World War II. While it faced challenges in terms of armor and firepower, its mobility, adaptability, and role in early war victories underscore its importance in the context of Japanese military history.

Soviet T-34 Tank

The Soviet T-34 tank emerged as a formidable force on the Eastern Front during World War II, leaving an indelible mark on military history. Renowned for its groundbreaking design, the T-34 played a pivotal role in the Soviet Union's defense against the German invasion, demonstrating exceptional versatility and combat effectiveness.

One of the T-34's key strengths lay in its innovative armor design. Unlike many contemporary tanks, the T-34 featured sloped armor, which significantly enhanced its defensive capabilities. The sloping design increased the effective thickness of the armor, providing superior protection against enemy fire. This feature not only made the T-34 more resilient on the battlefield but also influenced the design of future tanks.

Equipped with a powerful 76.2mm F-34 main gun, the T-34 boasted impressive firepower. The F-34 gun was effective against both enemy tanks and infantry, offering a well-balanced solution for a wide range of combat scenarios. The T-34's main gun, coupled with its sloped armor, gave it a considerable advantage over German tanks, often allowing Soviet crews to engage the enemy from positions of relative safety.

Mobility was another key asset of the T-34. Its robust engine and well-designed suspension system enabled the tank to traverse various terrains with ease. This mobility not only facilitated rapid maneuvers on the battlefield but also allowed the T-34 to outmaneuver slower and less agile enemy tanks. The combination of firepower, armor, and mobility made the T-34 a formidable adversary, contributing significantly to the Soviet Union's success in key battles.

The T-34's success was not solely attributed to its technical specifications but also to its production strategy. The Soviet Union adopted a pragmatic approach, focusing on mass production and simplicity in design. This strategy allowed the

T-34 to be produced in large numbers, quickly replacing losses suffered in the early stages of the war. The ability to field a substantial number of tanks played a crucial role in the Soviet Union's ability to withstand the German onslaught and eventually turn the tide of the conflict.

The T-34's impact extended beyond its immediate military capabilities. Its design influenced subsequent tank development worldwide, emphasizing the importance of sloped armor and balanced firepower. The tank's success also highlighted the significance of effective logistics and mass production in modern warfare.

Despite its undeniable strengths, the T-34 was not without its flaws. Early models faced issues with mechanical reliability, and crews often struggled with the tank's cramped interior. However, ongoing modifications and improvements addressed many of these concerns, enhancing the overall performance of the T-34 as the war progressed.

In conclusion, the Soviet T-34 tank played a crucial role in shaping the outcome of World War II on the Eastern Front. Its innovative design, formidable firepower, and strategic production approach made it a symbol of Soviet resilience and determination. The T-34's legacy endures not only in the annals of military history but also in the continued influence of its design principles on tank development worldwide.

The Eagles Nest

The Eagle's Nest, known as Kehlsteinhaus in German, was a mountaintop retreat commissioned by Adolf Hitler and located in the Bavarian Alps near the town of Berchtesgaden, Germany. Perched atop the Kehlstein mountain at an elevation of approximately 1,834 meters (6,017 feet), the Eagle's Nest offered awe-inspiring panoramic views of the surrounding landscape. Constructed between 1937 and 1938, the building served as a symbol of Hitler's power and was intended to be a place where he could relax, entertain guests, and showcase the grandiosity of the Nazi regime.

The idea for The Eagle's Nest was conceived by Martin Bormann, one of Hitler's closest associates. Construction of the retreat involved substantial effort and resources. A steep, winding mountain road was carved into the rocky slopes to provide access to the site. From the road's end, visitors would proceed via a specially designed elevator that would take them directly to the teahouse's entrance. The Eagle's Nest was designed to convey Hitler's perceived supremacy, with luxurious features such as a grand fireplace, rich wood paneling, and extravagant furnishings.

Despite its lavish appearance, The Eagle's Nest was not used extensively by Hitler himself. He reportedly visited the retreat only a few times due to his fear of heights and a preference for other residences, such as the Berghof located nearby in Obersalzberg. However, The Eagle's Nest did serve as a diplomatic venue, hosting foreign dignitaries and diplomats during the Nazi regime.

During World War II, The Eagle's Nest was not targeted by Allied bombings due to its remote location and relatively minor strategic importance. It remained largely intact throughout the war. As the conflict came to an end, the site was seized by American forces on May 5, 1945. The capture of The Eagle's Nest by the U.S. 101st Airborne Division and the 3rd Infantry Division marked the end of the Battle of Berchtesgaden, a campaign aimed at capturing strategic points in the region.

After the war, The Eagle's Nest was transformed into a recreation center for American troops stationed in the area. However, its association with the Nazi regime led to debates about its fate. In 1952, the Bavarian state government assumed control of the property and opened it to the public as a tourist attraction.

Today, The Eagle's Nest remains a popular destination for visitors from around the world. Tourists can access the site by buses from Obersalzberg, where they can learn about the building's history and the dark legacy of the Nazi regime through informative exhibits within the teahouse.

Efforts have been made to ensure that The Eagle's Nest serves as a place of historical remembrance, rather than glorification. The site's management and tour guides emphasize the importance of reflecting on the past and learning from history to prevent similar atrocities from happening in the future. By exploring The Eagle's Nest, visitors are reminded of the stark contrast between the breathtaking natural surroundings and the grim history that unfolded within its walls, urging them to strive for a more tolerant and compassionate world.

The Enigma Machine

During World War II, the Enigma Machine played a crucial role in the realm of secret communication. Developed by Germany, this ingenious device was used to encrypt and decrypt messages, providing a high level of secrecy for military communications. The Enigma Machine gave the Germans an advantage by safeguarding their messages, but its eventual decryption by the Allies, including the United States, marked a significant turning point in the war.

The Enigma Machine served as a complex encryption tool that scrambled messages into seemingly random combinations of letters and numbers. These encrypted messages were sent via radio or telegraph, making it difficult for intercepting forces to understand the content without the corresponding decryption key. This encryption method provided the Germans with a secure means of communication, allowing them to coordinate military actions and strategies without fear of interception.

The benefits of the Enigma Machine for the Germans were substantial. By encrypting their messages, they could convey important information across vast distances without revealing their intentions to the enemy. This element of surprise allowed the Germans to maintain a strategic advantage, catching their opponents off guard and potentially influencing the outcome of battles.

The story of the Enigma Machine took a turn when the United States obtained one of these devices. This acquisition was facilitated by a combination of intelligence efforts, espionage, and strategic captures of German equipment. Possessing an Enigma Machine allowed the Allies, including the US, to gain firsthand insight into how the encryption worked and how messages were encoded.

Breaking the code of the Enigma Machine was a significant achievement that altered the course of the war. It was the brilliant minds at Bletchley Park, a British codebreaking center, who made the pivotal breakthrough. Alan Turing, along with a team of dedicated cryptanalysts, devised sophisticated methods to decode the encrypted messages produced by the Enigma Machine.

The significance of deciphering Enigma-encrypted messages cannot be overstated. By cracking the code, the Allies gained access to critical German military plans, troop movements, and strategies. This allowed them to anticipate enemy actions, adjust their own plans accordingly, and sometimes even mislead the Germans by feeding them misinformation. The decrypted messages provided a clear view into the enemy's intentions, providing a strategic edge that contributed to the Allies' successes on the battlefield.

In conclusion, the Enigma Machine was a remarkable encryption device used by the Germans during World War II to secure their communication. Its complex encryption methods gave them a significant advantage, allowing them to maintain secrecy in their military operations. The acquisition of an Enigma Machine by the United States and the subsequent breaking of its code by Allied cryptanalysts, including Alan Turing, were pivotal moments in the war. The ability to read encrypted messages provided the Allies with invaluable insights and allowed them to make more informed decisions, ultimately contributing to their victory. The Enigma Machine's significance lies in its role as a symbol of the power of intelligence, innovation, and collaboration in overcoming even the most advanced challenges of warfare.

Shoichi Yokoi

Shoichi Yokoi was a Japanese soldier who gained international attention for his extraordinary survival story during and after World War II. Born on March 31, 1915, in Saori, Aichi, Japan, Yokoi became an unwitting symbol of endurance and resilience.

Yokoi's life took a dramatic turn when he was conscripted into the Imperial Japanese Army in 1941 during the early stages of World War II. As part of the 38th Infantry Division, he was deployed to the Pacific island of Guam in 1943. However, in 1944, the tide of the war shifted, and the American forces successfully invaded the island, leading to the capture or death of many Japanese soldiers, but Yokoi managed to escape.

Realizing the dire situation, Yokoi made the fateful decision to go into hiding in the dense jungle of Guam, determined to evade capture by the enemy forces. For the next 28 years, he lived in isolation, adapting to the harsh conditions of the jungle with remarkable resourcefulness.

During his extended period of seclusion, Yokoi's survival skills were put to the test. He constructed primitive shelters using bamboo and leaves, fashioned clothing from tree bark, and sustained himself by foraging for food and hunting small animals. Yokoi's ability to adapt to the unforgiving environment showcased his tenacity and will to survive.

Despite the passage of time, Yokoi remained vigilant, fearing the potential threat of enemy soldiers and steadfastly holding on to his duty as a soldier. His commitment to the military code and discipline helped him endure the solitude and hardships of his clandestine existence.

In January 1972, Yokoi's life took an unexpected turn when two local fishermen discovered him in the Talofofo River. His discovery made headlines worldwide, and the world marveled at the tale of a soldier who had survived for nearly three decades in isolation. Yokoi's stoic demeanor and survival skills captured the imagination of the public, turning him into a symbol of endurance.

Upon his return to Japan, Yokoi faced a mix of astonishment and admiration. His story became a testament to the strength of the human spirit and the lengths one could go to fulfill a sense of duty. Yokoi's experiences were documented in his book, "Private Yokoi's War: A Memoir and Manifesto," where he shared the details of his incredible journey.

Shoichi Yokoi's life post-return was marked by a combination of acclaim and adjustment. He struggled to reintegrate into a rapidly modernizing Japan, grappling with the changes that had occurred during his long absence. Despite the challenges, he became a symbol of resilience and determination, reminding the world of the indomitable human spirit.

Shoichi Yokoi's extraordinary story serves as a powerful testament to the human capacity for survival in the face of adversity. His legacy endures as a reminder of the strength inherent in the human spirit and the unyielding commitment to duty that guided him through years of isolation in the jungles of Guam.

Japanese Internment Camps

Japanese Internment Camps during World War II were a deeply controversial and distressing chapter in American history. These camps were the result of a combination of wartime fear, prejudice, and executive orders that led to the forced relocation and internment of Japanese Americans, regardless of their citizenship status.

In response to the attack on Pearl Harbor in December 1941, a wave of anti-Japanese sentiment swept across the United States. Fueled by fears of espionage and sabotage, President Franklin D. Roosevelt signed Executive Order 9066 in February 1942, which authorized the removal of Japanese Americans from the West Coast. This marked the beginning of a dark period characterized by the establishment of internment camps.

Approximately 120,000 Japanese Americans, two-thirds of whom were U.S. citizens, were uprooted from their homes and communities and relocated to ten internment camps scattered across the country. These camps were situated in remote and desolate areas, often lacking proper infrastructure and basic amenities. Families were given only a short notice to pack their belongings and were forced to abandon homes, businesses, and possessions.

Life in the internment camps was marked by harsh living conditions and loss of personal freedoms. Barracks were overcrowded and lacked privacy, with families often cramped into single rooms. Basic necessities such as food, clothing, and medical care were often inadequate. Barbed wire fences and guard towers were a constant reminder of the loss of liberty. Despite these hardships, Japanese Americans in the camps sought to maintain a sense of community, establishing schools, churches, and recreational activities.

The internment camps had a profound impact on the individuals and families who were unjustly detained. Loss of property, education, and career opportunities took a toll on their lives and futures. The emotional and psychological trauma of being forcibly uprooted and confined under suspicion and prejudice had long-lasting effects on many.

The internment camps' significance lies in their violation of civil liberties and the principles of justice and equality enshrined in the Constitution. The internment was widely criticized even at the time, with civil rights organizations, religious leaders, and citizens condemning the government's actions. In 1988, the U.S. government formally acknowledged the injustice and signed the Civil Liberties Act, providing an official apology and reparations to surviving internees.

The legacy of Japanese Internment Camps serves as a reminder of the dangers of unchecked prejudice and the erosion of civil liberties during times of crisis. The internment experience remains a cautionary tale that underscores the importance of upholding constitutional rights, protecting minority communities, and challenging discrimination.

In conclusion, Japanese Internment Camps during World War II were a painful manifestation of wartime fear and prejudice. These camps forcibly relocated and interned Japanese Americans, resulting in loss of liberty, property, and opportunities. The harsh conditions and violation of civil rights in the camps underscore the importance of safeguarding individual freedoms even in times of crisis. The legacy of Japanese internment serves as a somber reminder of the need to uphold justice, equality, and the protection of all citizens' rights.

Made in United States
Orlando, FL
18 June 2024